# WORDPRESS
# BLOCK THEME

Everything you need to know to create a block theme

2026, Roy Sahupala

## Important note

The methods and programs in this manual are stated without regard to any patents. They are for amateur and study purposes only. All technical data and programs in this book were compiled by the author with the greatest care and reproduced after thorough checking. Nevertheless, errors cannot be completely excluded. The publisher is therefore forced to point out that it can assume neither any warranty nor any legal responsibility or any form of liability for consequences arising from erroneous information. The reporting of any errors is always appreciated by the author.

Please be advised that the software and hardware names mentioned in this book, as well as the brand names of the companies involved are mostly protected by manufacturer's marks, trademarks or by patent law.

Author:         R.E. Sahupala
ISBN/EAN:       9798326141774
First edition:  14-06-2024
Edition:        01-26 KDP
NUR code:       994
Publisher:      WJAC
Website:        www.wp-books.com/block-theme

With special thanks to:
My dear wife Iris van Hattum and our son Ebbo Sahupala.

# INDEX

# INTRODUCTION

As of WordPress 5.0, it uses a **block editor** called the name **Gutenberg**. This makes it possible to easily add formatting and style to **pages** and **posts**.

As of 2022, there are two types of themes: **classic** and **block themes**. As of version 5.9, WordPress uses for the first time a block theme called **Twenty Twenty-Two**.

Customizing **classic themes** is done with the Dashboard **Customizer**. If you have knowledge of HTML, CSS and PHP, you can also make changes under the hood.

Customizing a **block theme** is done using a **site editor**. This allows a user to visually modify the layout and style of a theme without requiring knowledge of HTML, CSS and PHP.

After a block theme is activated, the site editor can be found in the Dashboard. Customization is done using the same interface for pages and posts. It allows a user to edit, move, add or remove theme blocks such as a Title, Logo, Navigation and Widgets, as well as adjust styles such as color, size and font.

It is also possible to use the editor to create **patterns**, custom **templates** and template **components**, and change the layout structure of a homepage, post or page.

WordPress calls this **Full Site Editing**.

Using Full Site Editing, an administrator is no longer dependent on a developer or designer to make changes to a theme. It is even possible to use the Editor to create a block theme.

As of 2023 version 6.0, the Editor is officially released, but after collection of feedback, changes may still occur.

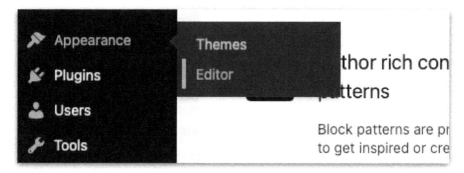

If you want to be ready for the future, this book is a great start to getting acquainted with **Full Site Editing** and **block themes**.

# CLASSIC AND BLOCK THEME

A **classic theme** allows you, as the theme creator, to determine what a user may customize using the Customizer. This keeps a user within the boundaries of a theme style.

If you are creating a website for an organization with a fixed style and layout, and if a user is only allowed to provide content, then you can use a classic theme for this purpose. It consists mainly of PHP and CSS files.

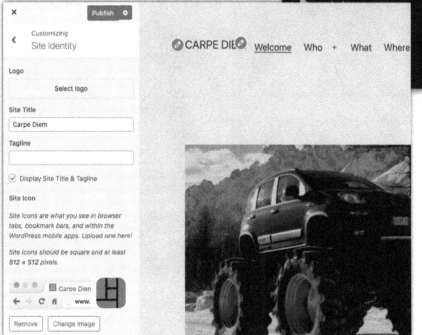

A **block theme** allows a user to change the layout structure within a theme style. This can be done by repositioning **theme blocks**, such as a navigation, title and content block.

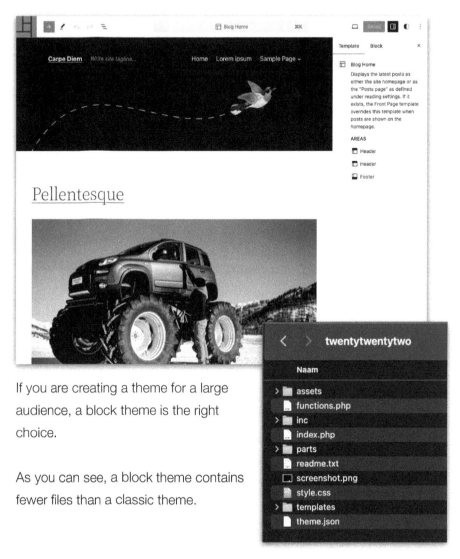

If you are creating a theme for a large audience, a block theme is the right choice.

As you can see, a block theme contains fewer files than a classic theme.

Here is an overview of the two types of themes.

## Classic theme

▸ File structure consists of mostly PHP files.

▸ Layout is predetermined.

▸ A select number of components can be customized.

▸ Customization is done with **Dashboard > Appearance > Customize**.

▸ Contains more code and files than a block theme.

▸ Is made to guard the theme style.

▸ HTML, CSS and PHP knowledge is required to create a theme.

▸ There are more than ten thousand themes available.

## Block theme

▸ File structure consists of HTML and a JSON file.

▸ Layout is predetermined.

▸ Customization is done with **Dashboard > Appearance > Editor**.

▸ The layout can be changed visually.

▸ Each theme block can be customized.

▸ Dashboard components such as *Customize*, *Menus* and *Widgets* have been replaced by the site editor.

▸ The Gutenberg user interface is included in the site editor.

▸ No code is required to customize a theme.

▸ A user can create additional theme files, such as a pattern, template or part, among others.

▸ Contains less code and files than a classic theme.

▸ Is made to customize theme style and layout.

▸ You don't need HTML and CSS knowledge to create a block theme.

▸ More than seven hundred block themes available.

# WHY A BLOCK THEME

The Gutenberg block editor is now found throughout the Dashboard, creating a unified interface. Since version 5.9, users can also customize a block theme using the same editor as for a page or post. Classic themes are not suitable for this, which is why WordPress opted for a new theme format.

Due to the large number of existing classic themes, it will be some time before they are no longer supported.

## What types of themes are available?

Theme creators are currently busy developing block themes. It is also possible to create combinations of both types. The following is an overview of the types available:

**Classic themes**
Themes consisting of PHP template files and functions.php.

**Hybrid themes**
Classic themes that support Full Site Editing, such as block settings, patterns and templates.

**Universal themes**
Block themes with classic components managed through the Dashboard Customizer, such as menus and widgets.

**Block themes**
Themes created for Full Site Editing.

# PURPOSE OF THIS BOOK

This book explains how a block theme works, how to customize it and how to create one yourself. The book contains only the most essential explanations. After gaining enough experience, you will gain more insight and confidence to expand and create block themes independently.

This book is written for anyone who wants to work quickly and practically with block themes, without requiring HTML, CSS and PHP knowledge. In addition, the method described provides insight into how a block theme is created.

All theme files used in this book are available at:
**wp-books.com/block-theme**.
The password can be found on page 70.

Check the site frequently for additional information.

All the exercises in this book are practical. I show only the most essential, it contains no unnecessary description and is immediately applicable.

Explanations for MacOS and Windows users.

**Tip: take your time! Read a chapter carefully before taking a seat at the computer.**

# WHO IS THIS BOOK FOR?

Using this book it is possible to create a block theme independently. Code knowledge is not required, but it is helpful if you have basic knowledge of HTML and CSS.

This book is for:
▸ WordPress users with a basic knowledge of WordPress.
▸ WordPress users who do not want to depend on developers.
▸ WordPress users who want to create or extend a block theme.

## What do you need to create a block theme?

The latest version of WordPress. A text editor for editing code, such as Teksteditor (Apple) or NotePad (Windows).

If you regularly work with code, you can also use a **code editor**.
There are several open source code editors available such as Atom. Go to *https://github.com/atom/atom/releases/tag/v1.60.0* for more information.

Want to use another code editor? Then search Google for "free open-source code editors."

To connect to your Web site, you need an **Internet browser**. It is recommended that you install more than one browser. If a certain WordPress feature does not work in your favorite browser, you can quickly switch to another browser. All exercises in this book have been tested with the latest versions of Firefox, Safari, Chrome and Edge.

The program **LOCAL** allows you to install WordPress on your own computer. After the installation, you have immediate access to all your theme files. The site folder can be found in the user folder of Windows or MacOS.
Go to: **user folder > Local sites > Name site > app > public**.

You can find more information about the LOCAL program in the book **WordPress - Basics**. Or go to *localwp.com*.

If you are using the program **MAMP**, you will find the files in the folder **Apps > MAMP > htdocs > Name site**. More information: *mamp.com*.

If you installed WordPress using a web host, you can use an **FTP** program to access your theme files.

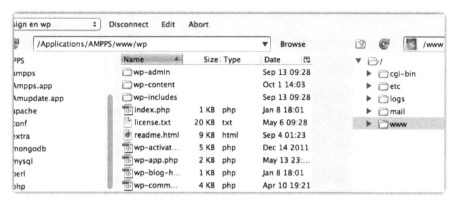

There are several free FTP programs available, such as **FileZilla** or **Cyberduck**.

You can place a block theme in the **themes** folder of your WordPress site. See: **wp-content > themes**.

If you want to know more about WordPress, I would like to refer you to my other books:

**WordPress - Basic.**
**WordPress - Advanced.**
**WordPress - WooCommerce.**
**WordPress - Classic Theme.**
**WordPress - Gutenberg.**

# ATOMIC DESIGN

WordPress has chosen a design philosophy that allows you to create a website with the smallest element. This is in contrast to other methods that often have a top down approach. This principle is called **Atomic Design**. With the Gutenberg project, it is intended to implement this method not only in Pages or Posts, but throughout the WordPress system.

In the future, Gutenberg will allow a user to format not only pages and posts, but also the layouts of plugins, widgets and even themes.

## Design method

Atomic design assumes the smallest element as the building block. It is a modular system. With building blocks you create site components. By combining them, you create templates that you can incorporate into pages.

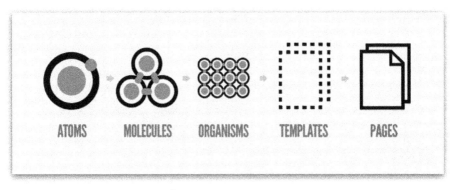

A bottom up approach, from simple to complex. Components that are assembled can be broken down and built up quickly. It's a lot like Lego ... We're going to look at the five design components.

## Atoms

Atoms are basic components such as titles, paragraphs, buttons, quotes, columns and tables.

## Molecules

Groups of atoms are called molecules. Here you can think of elements such as a cover block, media and text, a call to action and a gallery.

## Organisms

Constructions consisting of atoms and molecules are called organisms. These are intended for a specific purpose within a page.
Here you can think of a header, section, separator and footer.

## Templates

Templates are organisms that take up the entire width of a page.
This is also called template.

## Pages

The aggregate of all the components forms a page. It contains components such as a header, navigation menu, sections, templates, sidebars and a footer. A page can be quickly and easily broken down and reassembled for other purposes.

## Atomic design in WordPress

The smallest basic element in WordPress is a **Block**. With a block you can create page elements, also called **Patterns**. With several patterns, you can format an entire page, also called a **Template**. The whole thing is placed in a Theme, or Page. Together they form a responsive whole that adapts to different screen sizes.

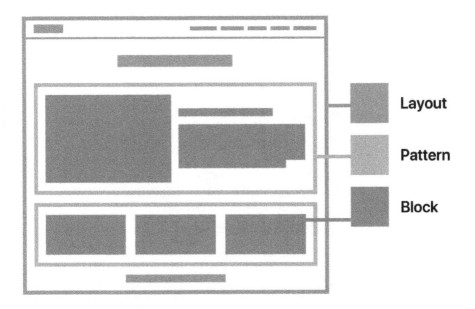

Blocks are individual elements.

Patterns consist of layout elements.

Template is the complete page layout.

Theme consists of several page layouts.

Based on this design principle, the layout of a theme can be built.

# BLOCK THEME

Before we start creating a block theme, it's helpful to see how it works and what's available. As of version 5.9, WordPress uses the first block theme, called **Twenty Twenty-Two**.

Install WordPress and go to **Dashboard > Appearance**.
**Install** and **activate** the **Twenty Twenty-Two** theme.

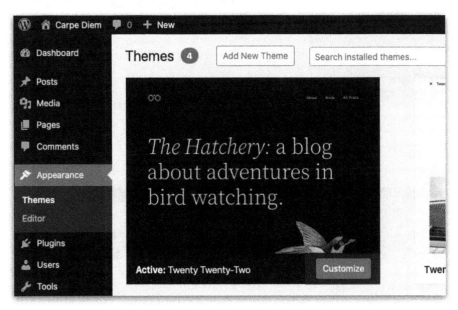

With this theme, WordPress wants to show how easy it is to customize a block theme. When a block theme is activated, **Customize**, **Widgets** and **Menus** are replaced by **Editor**.

When a classic theme is activated, the above menu items are back in the Dashboard.

Go to **Appearance > Editor**. The Site Editor appears. In the left column you'll see a number of options: **Navigation**, **Styles**, **Pages**, **Templates** and **Patterns**. On the right you'll see the homepage with the latest posts.

Select the **title**, then click **Edit Template**.
A **toolbar** will appear above the block.

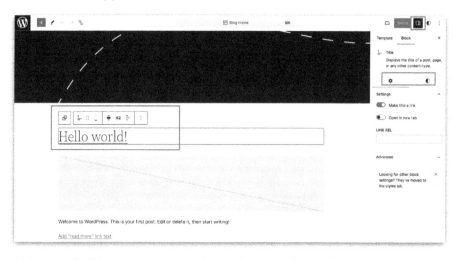

Using the **Settings** icon (top right), you'll find additional **block options** in a right-hand column. With **Block Settings** (gear icon) and **Styles** (crescent icon), you can further customize the block.

The **WordPress** icon (top left) will take you back to the Site Editor.

Navigate to **Appearance > Editor - Templates**. Templates consist of template parts and blocks, which together form a page. A template part could be a **Header**, **Sidebar**, or **Footer**. A template typically consists of multiple parts.

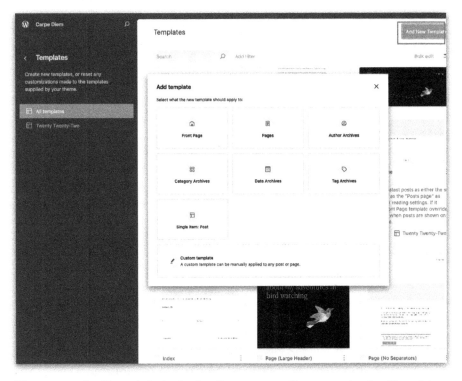

The name of a **Template** indicates its purpose. For example, the Template **Single Posts** is displayed when a visitor clicks on a post from the home-page, showing the entire post. The number of templates may vary depen-ding on the theme.

You can create new templates by clicking **Add New Template**.

Select **Single Posts** and click on a **block** to edit it.

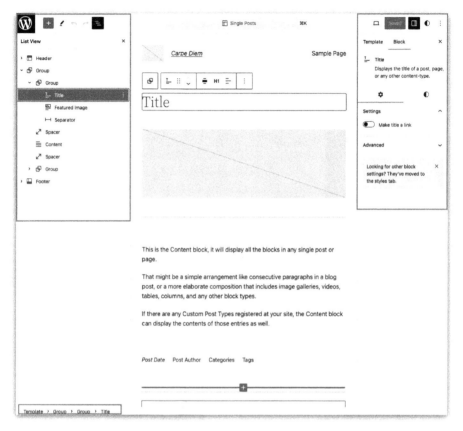

The structure of a template consists of **template parts** and **theme blocks**. By selecting a template component or block, you can see its function. You can do this either by using **List View** or **breadcrumbs**.

Adjust block settings using the **block options** and **styles** in the right column.

You can add template parts and theme blocks using the block inserter, represented by the ➕ icon at the top left.

Go to **Appearance > Editor > Patterns**. Alongside theme Patterns (layouts), you'll also find a list of TEMPLATE PARTS. Click on a Part to edit it.

The name indicates the type it represents.

Using **Add New Patterns > Add New Template Part** allows you to create template parts.

The benefit of working with a **Template Part** is that it enables you to focus on the layout without being overwhelmed by the entire page structure.

## Edit Homepage, Template and Template Parts

With the Gutenberg Site Editor, you can seamlessly add or modify Blocks and Patterns, and changes take effect immediately upon saving. Once a Template or Template Part is altered, it is indicated in the Template over-view, accessible via **Templates > All templates >** *Template* **- Actions** (three dots). By selecting **Reset**, you can clear customizations.

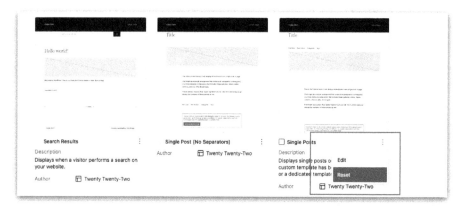

To illustrate, let's proceed to edit a template.
Navigate to **Editor > Templates** and select the **Single Posts** template.

Our objective is to substitute the Header and Footer with a Pattern. Additionally, we'll adjust the Meta information blocks, including Date, Author, and Category, positioned directly below the Title.

**Header and Footer customization:**

1. Navigate to **List View** and select the **Group** within the **Header**.
2. Click on the **+** icon and opt for **Patterns**.
3. Select the **Headers** category.
4. Select **Text-only header with tagline and background**.
5. **Delete** the **old Group**.
6. Adjust Text and Link color to white.

Repeat the same process for the **footer**, selecting **Dark footer with title and citation**.

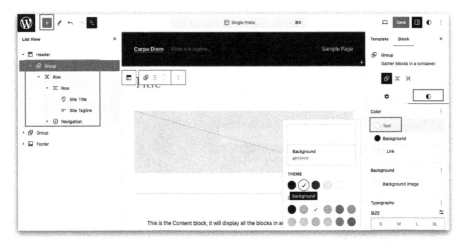

Then, move the *Meta information* directly below the **Title** by **selecting** and **dragging** the Meta information **row** under the **Title**.

Utilize the **List View** tool for assistance. Next, adjust the width to **Wide Width**. **Save** your changes and preview a post.

Refer to the **WordPress Gutenberg** book for more insight into layouts and full site editing.

## Navigation menu

First, **publish three pages**. Then go to the Site **Editor** and **select** the **Navigation** block. From Block Settings (right column) - **Menu**, click on the three dots and select **Create New Menu**.

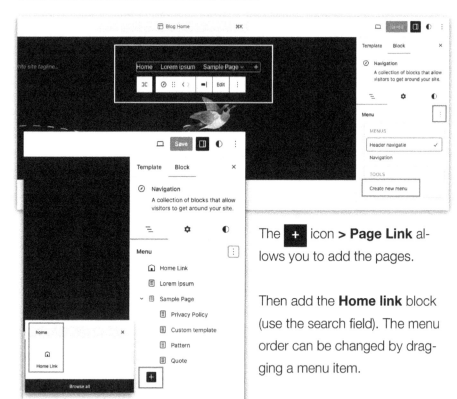

The  icon > **Page Link** allows you to add the pages.

Then add the **Home link** block (use the search field). The menu order can be changed by dragging a menu item.

Select a menu item to add a **Submenu** (3 dots).

Then **Save** the template.

## Add Template

If you are missing a template, for example the template *Full Width*, *With Sidebar* or *Homepage*, you can create it with the site editor. No plugin or code is required for this. After a **Custom template** is created you get to decide how it is constructed.

From a **Page** or **Post** you can specify if you want to use this.

### A new template

Go to **Dashboard > Page > Sample Page** (or any other page).
Go to the right column - **Page** tab **> Template - Pages**.

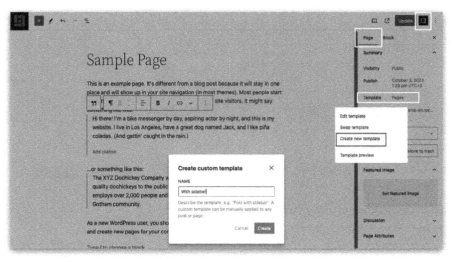

Select **Create new template**. A popup window appears where you can enter a template name. Give the custom template the name **With sidebar**.

Then click **Create**.

The **site editor** is activated. From here, you can build the layout of the custom template. Use the available **blocks** and **patterns** to do this.

As you can see, the **Columns** block has been used. In the left column you place a **Content** block, in the right column a **Calendar** block.
The **Columns** block is placed in the **Group** block.

The structure can be seen using **List View**. After you are done, click the **Update** and **Save** button. Using the **< Back** button (top), you get to see the **Page** again.

The right column shows that the template **With sidebar** is being used. **Edit Template** allows you to modify the template.

The template can also be found in the **Site Editor**. Go to: **Dashboard > Appearance > Editor - Templates.**

View the site.

## Edit custom template

The page with the template **With sidebar** is applied. There is no template component such as a **header** and **footer** included in the template.

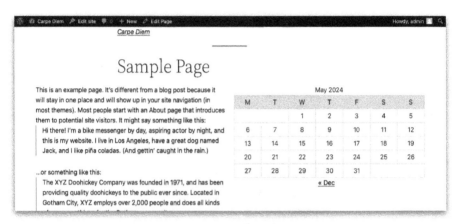

If you want to use default **Template Parts**, you may customize the template.

Go to **Dashboard > Appearance > Editor > Templates > All Templates - With sidebar**. Click to **Edit**.

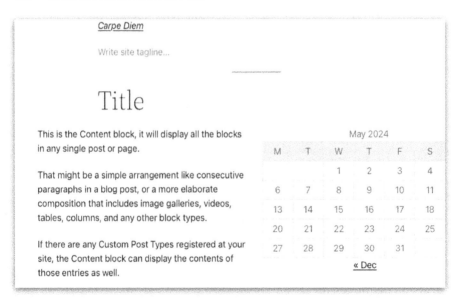

Click on the **+** icon and select **Patterns > Headers > simple header with dark background**.

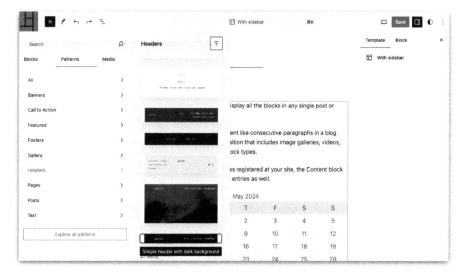

Then select **Patterns > Footer > Dark footer with title and citation**.

Use **List View** to view structure the layout.

At the top of the template remove the **Group** with *Site title* and *Tagline*.

Drag the pattern **Header** to the top, the **Footer** at the bottom.

After that, click **Save**.

There are additional actions after that to make sure the template fits the theme better.

You may also add the **Featured Image** block.

The **Columns** block is placed in a **Group**.

Select the **Group** block and go to block settings (right column).

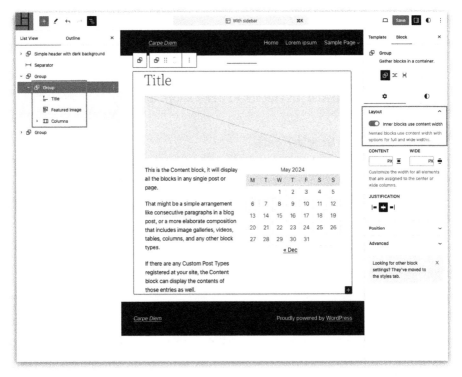

At **Layout**, activate **Inner blocks use content width**.

Nested blocks use this to fill the width of this container.

If you want to know more about theme block properties, these can be found in the Templates **Pages** or **Single Posts**.

Then click **Save** and view the page.

## Reuse default layout

If you want to use the layout of a default template in a custom template then you can use the layout of a default template. It is then no longer necessary to add a header and footer to the custom template.

Go to the template **Single Posts**.
From the right column **Options** (3 dots) select **Code editor**.

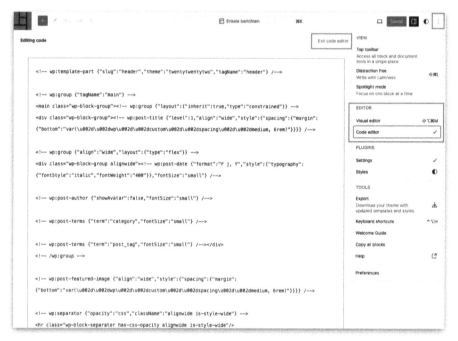

**Copy** the entire code and **paste** it into the custom template **With sidebar**. This will overwrite the formatting. After that, don't forget to return to the **Visual editor**.

After the custom template is saved you can customize it with additional blocks such as a **Group**, **Columns** and **Calendar**.

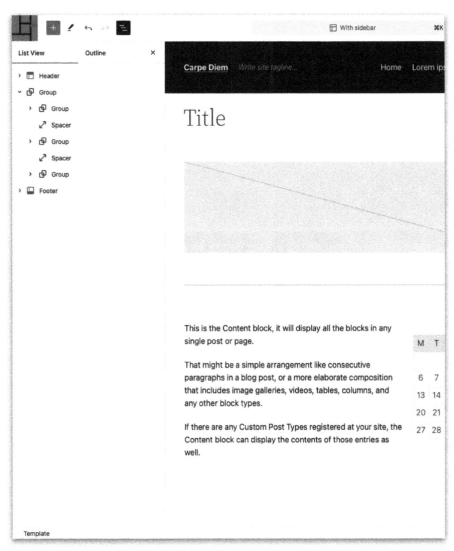

Using **List View**, you can see how the template has been customized.

# THEME BLOCKS

After activating a block theme, menu items **Widgets** and **Menus** are no longer included in the **Dashboard**.

Widgets and theme blocks are added in a block theme using the **site editor**. A user gets to decide in which template and position this is placed. In a classic theme, such elements have a fixed position.

## Widget blocks

Default widget blocks have been included in the page editor since version 5.8 and can also be seen in the site editor.

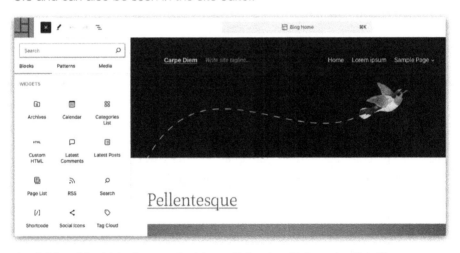

Available widget blocks are: Archives, Calendar, Categories list, Own HTML, Newest comments, Newest posts, Page list, RSS, Search, Shortcode, Social icons and Tag cloud.

Go to **Dashboard > Appearance > Editor > Templates - Blog home** and click on **Edit**. Hover your cursor over a widget block and you will see a preview.

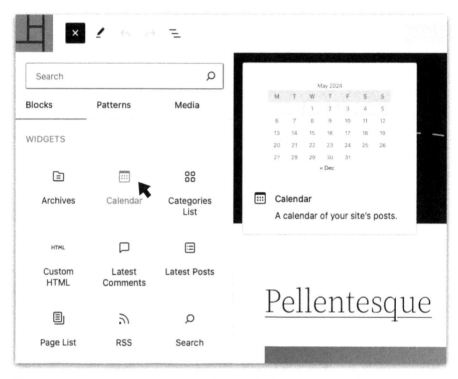

You may place a widget anywhere in the block theme. In a classic theme, it is only possible to place a widget in a designated area, such as a sidebar or footer.

A widget block can also be inserted into a page or post.

## Theme blocks

Using the block-inserter ⊞ , a number of **Theme** blocks can be seen.

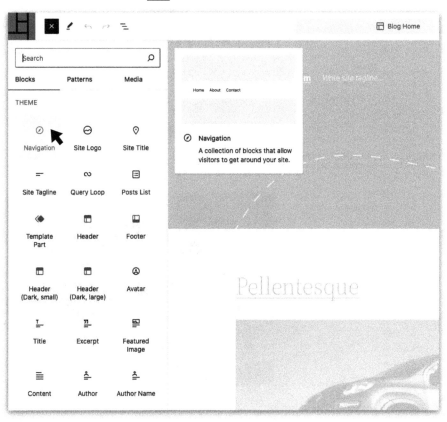

Available theme blocks are: Navigation, Site logo, -Title and -Tagline, Query Loop, Posts list, Template Part, Header, Footer, Avatar, Title, Excerpt, Featured Image, Content, Author, Date, Categories, Tags, Next and Previous post, Read More, Comments, Login/Out, Term Description, Archive title and Search Result Title.

If you hover the cursor over a topic block, you will see a preview. The **List view** allows you to see which blocks a template consists of.

WordPress - Block Theme

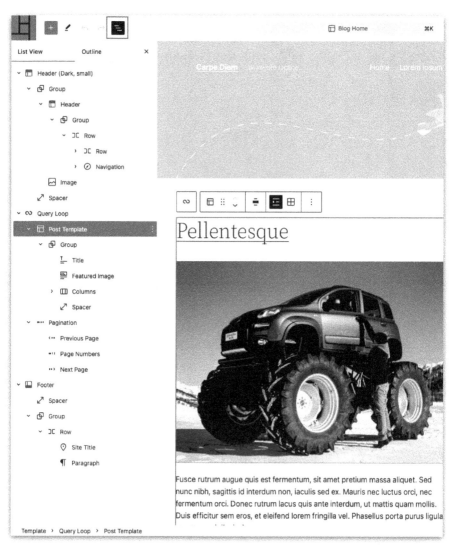

With theme blocks, you control the layout of a web page. You have the same freedom to change, delete or move blocks as you would in a page editor.

# THEME PATTERNS

From the site editor, a theme has its own patterns. These consist of various composite theme blocks. These include Headers, Footers, Pages, Buttons, Columns, Text, etc.

With patterns, it is no longer necessary for a user to compose their own layout.

Click on the block-inserter ➕. Then select the **Patterns** tab. Patterns are divided into a number of categories: All, Banners, Call to action, Featured, Footers, Gallery, Headers, Pages, Posts, Text.

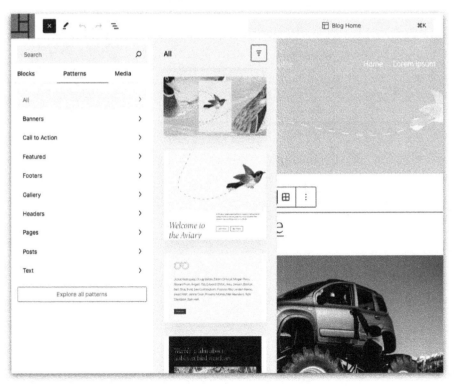

Make a selection, then the pattern is added to the template.

The **Explore all patterns** button will load the same categories in a popup window.

After a selection is made, it is added to the template.

The *Creating Patterns* chapter explains how to add patterns to a theme.

# GLOBAL STYLE

The design of a block theme is defined by a Web designer. In addition to a default layout, formatting and patterns, it is also decided what **global styles**, will be applied.

This includes styles for **typography**, **color** and **layout**. This style is also applied to editor blocks. Each theme has its own global style. Customizing a global style can be done using the **site editor**.

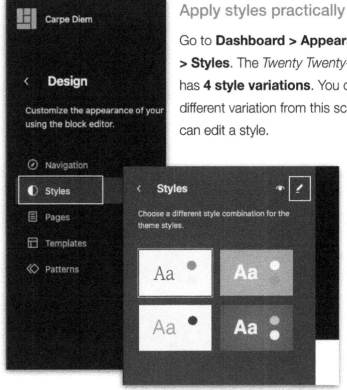

## Apply styles practically

Go to **Dashboard > Appearance > Editor > Styles**. The *Twenty Twenty-Two* theme has **4 style variations**. You can choose a different variation from this screen, or you can edit a style.

Click on the **Pencil** icon (Edit).

## Browse styles

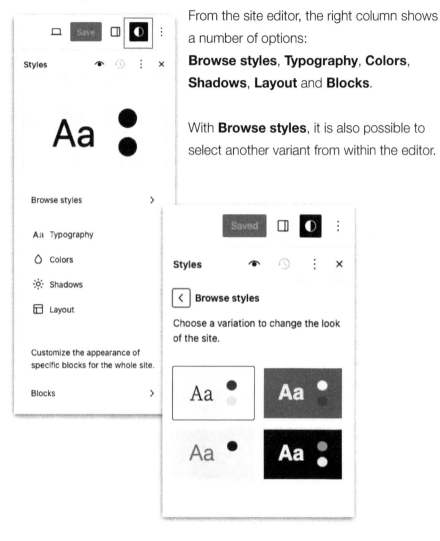

From the site editor, the right column shows a number of options:
**Browse styles**, **Typography**, **Colors**, **Shadows**, **Layout** and **Blocks**.

With **Browse styles**, it is also possible to select another variant from within the editor.

## Typography

The **Typography** panel allows you to customize styles for **Text**, **Links**, **Headings**, **Captions** and **Buttons**.

From the panel, select an **Element**.

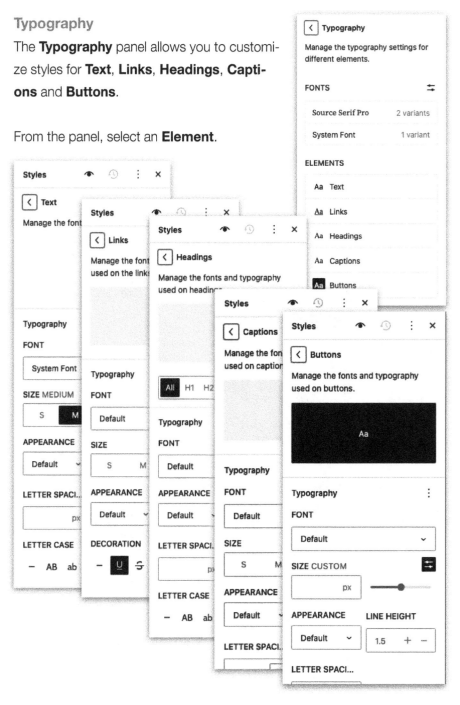

## Colors & Shadows

The Colors panel allows you to change **Palette**, **Text**, **Background**, **Link**, **Captions**, **Button** and **Heading** colors.

From the panel, select a **Color**.

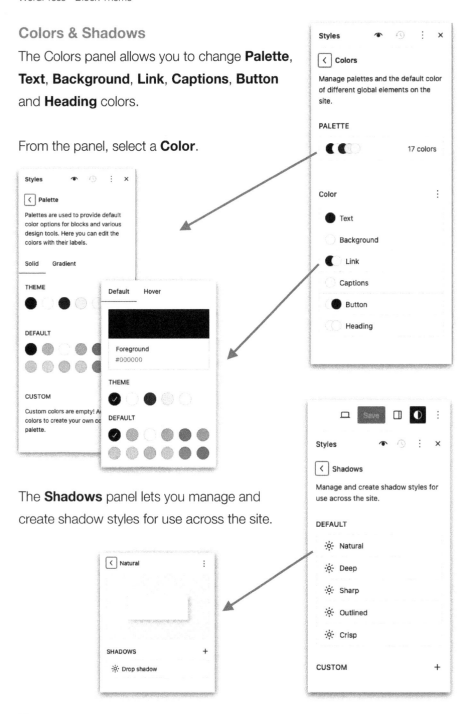

The **Shadows** panel lets you manage and create shadow styles for use across the site.

## Layout

With the **Layout** panel it is possible to adjust the **Padding** inside space of the theme,. This creates additional space within the theme.

Click on **Padding options** to specify a padding per side. Click on **px** to change units of measurement.

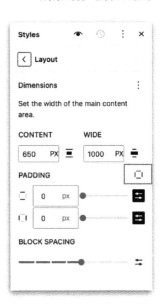

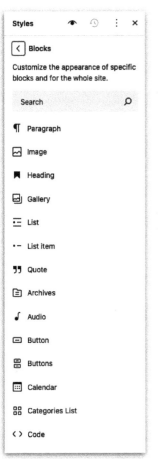

## Blocks

The **Blocks** panel allows you to customize the style of blocks.

Changes are applied throughout the site.

After inserting a block, it is still possible to modify it individually using the editor.

From this panel, select a block to change its overall style.

In this example, the **Paragraph** block was chosen.

The number of style options varies by block.

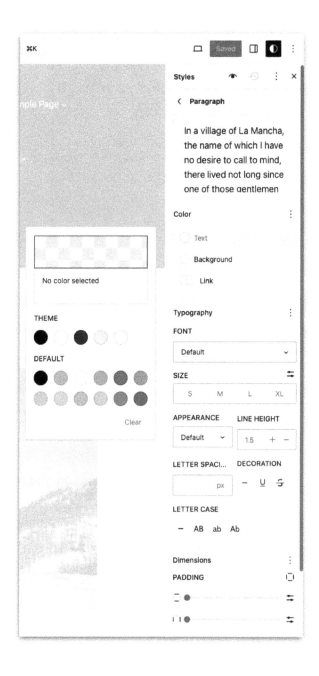

## Reset block styles

If the style of a block has been modified and you want to return to the default setting, go the **Blocks > Paragraph > Color** panel.

Using **Color options** (three dots), choose **Reset all**.

# WIDE WIDTH & FULL WIDTH

The block editor has new alignment options namely: **Wide width** and **Full width**. With these, a block uses the available width of a **theme** or browser **window**. Note! Not all themes support this. In that case, these options are not displayed.

The following is an overview of the blocks that use it:

| Text | Design | Embeds |
|------|--------|--------|
| Heading | Columns | All - unless contain- |
| Pullquote | Group, Row | ment is limited |
| Table | Separator | |

| Media | Widgets | Theme |
|-------|---------|-------|
| Image | Archive | Query Loop |
| Gallery | Calendar | Site - Title |
| Audio | Categories | - Content |
| Cover | Latest Comments | - Date |
| File | Latest Posts | - Excerpt |
| Media & Text | RSS | - Featured Image |
| Video | Tag Cloud | |

**Wide width** uses the full width of the theme. In most cases, a theme has a maximum width. If the site loads in a browser screen that is wider than the theme, the block gets the same width as the theme.

**Full width** uses the full width of a browser window. If the site loads in a window wider than the theme, the block will have the same width as the window.

**Full height** works only with a **Cover** block. This displays the full height of an image. You can combine this with Wide width and Full width.

The Twenty Twenty-One theme supports these options, see the example to the right. At the top you see a paragraph and image block, both centered. Below that, you see 3 columns of text and a wide-width image. At the very bottom there is a full-width and full-height image (see option - Full height).

Thanks to the new options, you are no longer bound to the default width of a page. This offers more space to, for example, use a cover block as a header or provide a page with 3 columns. It also allows you to place several blocks side by side. In short, it gives users more options to format pages and posts.

If you're going to use another theme, make sure the theme has both options. In the next chapter, I will show you how to place two or more default block elements side by side.

Lorem ipsum dolor sit amet, consectetur adipiscing elit. Donec consequat metus eu est laoreet rutrum. Vestibulum pharetra augue id lacus tristique, et feugiat diam ornare. Praesent finibus nibh dolor, vel vulputate eros fringilla vitae. Vestibulum lobortis tincidunt augue, et varius risus convallis quis. Proin dignissim faucibus eros, ut condimentum felis vehicula at. Nam vitae ligula ante. Quisque id congue risus. Duis ligula mi, ultricies fermentum interdum nec, laoreet in mauris.

(Centered)

Lorem ipsum dolor sit amet, consectetur adipiscing elit. Donec consequat metus eu est laoreet rutrum. Vestibulum pharetra augue id lacus tristique, et feugiat diam ornare. Praesent finibus nibh dolor, vel vulputate eros fringilla vitae. Vestibulum lobortis tincidunt augue, et varius risus convallis quis. Proin dignissim faucibus eros, ut condimentum felis vehicula at.

Proin non nisl nisi. In lectus nisi, imperdiet ac massa sit amet, sagittis elementum massa. Aliquam maximus a risus non bibendum. Curabitur semper tellus eu arcu blandit, vel venenatis tortor aliquet. Nunc volutpat urna mattis sem sagittis ultricies id vitae nunc. Nulla non ipsum a sem venenatis condimentum id eu odio. Donec finibus tortor a dolor cornelis viverra. Nulla vel est ac urna gravida posuere.

Vestibulum ante ipsum primis in faucibus orci luctus et ultrices posuere cubilia curae; Aenean ipsum urna, laoreet vitae ex a, aliquam efficitur ligula. Etiam aliquet risus ut dignissim imperdiet. Donec maximus in magna sit amet vulputate. In hac habitasse platea dictumst. Etiam vel diam id odio fringilla ullamcorper quis nec tortor. Praesent sapien turpis, tristique eget odio ut, viverra egestas nunc.

Wide width

Lorem ipsum dolor sit amet, consectetur adipiscing elit. Donec consequat metus eu est laoreet rutrum. Vestibulum pharetra augue id lacus tristique, et feugiat diam ornare. Praesent finibus nibh dolor, vel vulputate eros fringilla vitae. Vestibulum lobortis tincidunt augue, et varius risus convallis quis. Proin dignissim faucibus eros, ut condimentum felis vehicula at.

Proin non nisl nisi. In lectus nisi, imperdiet ac massa sit amet, sagittis elementum massa. Aliquam maximus a risus non bibendum. Curabitur semper tellus eu arcu blandit, vel venenatis tortor aliquet. Nunc volutpat urna mattis sem sagittis ultricies id vitae nunc. Nulla non ipsum a sem venenatis condimentum id eu odio. Donec finibus tortor a dolor cornelis viverra. Nulla vel est ac urna gravida posuere.

Vestibulum ante ipsum primis in faucibus orci luctus et ultrices posuere cubilia curae; Aenean ipsum urna, laoreet vitae ex a, aliquam efficitur ligula. Etiam aliquet risus ut dignissim imperdiet. Donec maximus in magna sit amet vulputate. In hac habitasse platea dictumst. Etiam vel diam id odio fringilla ullamcorper quis nec tortor. Praesent sapien turpis, tristique eget odio ut, viverra egestas nunc.

Full width

# THEME FILE STRUCTURE

What does a block theme consist of? After WordPress is installed on your own computer with the **Local** program, you have direct access to all your theme files. For Windows or MacOS users go to: **user folder > Local sites > site name > app > public > wp-content > themes**.

For **MAMP** users: **apps > MAMP > htdocs > site name > app > public > wp-content > themes**.

If you have installed WordPress online, you can use an **FTP** program to access your theme files.

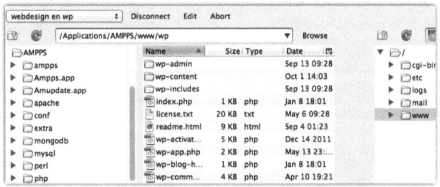

There are several free FTP programs available such as **FileZilla** or **Cyberduck**.

In the **themes** folder you will find the block theme **twentytwentytwo**.

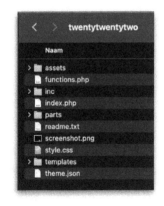

The file structure of a block theme (right) is different from a classic theme (left).

A classic theme such as **twentytwentytone** contains many more PHP and JavaScript files.

A block theme contains fewer PHP files. It primarily uses HTML and a JSON file.

More information about the file structure for block themes can be found in the Word-Press Theme Handbook: *https://developer.wordpress.org/themes/block-themes/block-theme-setup*.

To the right is an example of a file structure.

```
assets (dir)
        - css (dir)
                - blocks (dir)
        - images (dir)
        - js (dir)
inc (dir)
patterns (dir)
parts (dir)
        - footer.html
        - header.html
templates(dir)
        - 404.html
        - archive.html
        - index.html
        - page.html
        - single.html
        - search.html
functions.php
index.php
README.txt
rtl.css
screenshot.png
style.css
editor-style.css
theme.json
```

A default block theme consists of:

▸ **assets** - folder containing theme files such as images and fonts.

▸ **functions.php** - configuration and reference to theme files.

▸ **inc** - folder with pattern files such as:

  ▸ **block**-patterns.php - configuration block file.

  ▸ **patterns** - folder containing various pattern files such as:

    ▸ **header-default.php.**

    ▸ **header-large.php.**

    ▸ **header-small.php.**

    ▸ **etc.**

▸ **index.php** - not required as of version 6.0.

▸ **parts** - folder containing template parts such as:

  ▸ **header.html** - template containing a header block.

  ▸ **footer.html** - template containing a footer block.

  ▸ **sidebar.html** - template containing a sidebar block.

▸ **readme.txt** - theme information.

▸ **screenshot.png** - theme preview.

▸ **style.css** - theme style sheet.

▸ **styles** - folder containing additional JSON style files.

▸ **templates** - folder containing HTML files such as:

  ▸ **index.html** - template for a home page.

  ▸ **single.html** - template for a single post.

  ▸ **page.html** - template for a page.

▸ **theme.json** - configuration file for styling theme and blocks.

# PREPARATION THEME MAKING

Only a few files are needed to create a block theme. We start with a basic theme, which consists of a number of basic files. By editing templates and parts from the site editor, you can change the structure and style of the theme. When the theme is ready, you can export it and make it available to other users.

Using the **theme.json** file, you can add a common style to the theme. These can be found under the **settings** and **styles** categories.

```
1   {
2       "version": 2,
3 >     "settings": {=},
46 >    "styles": {=},
74 >    "templateParts": [=],
86 >    "customTemplates": [=]
93  }
```

Under the category **settings** you can include properties, under the category **styles** these are applied to various blocks and elements.

From the site editor, you mainly deal with **color**, **typography**, **layout**, **blocks**, **elements** and **parts** of them.

Before you begin, it is useful to first create a representation of the theme. Know what you are going to create. What are the dimensions of the theme? What will the header and footer look like? Will you use custom templates and what theme patterns will you use?

On the next page you will see some websites that can help you determine the right style.

## Layout

To determine the dimensions of a layout, you can use **Statcounter's** website. The goal of a theme is to fit within the desktop screen of a large number of visitors. In the North America, a screen resolution of **1920 x 1080 pixels** or higher is primarily used.

A block theme is responsive. The screen automatically adjusts when loaded on a tablet or smartphone.

In most block themes, the **ContentSize** is 650 to 1050 pixels and **wideSize** 1600 to 1240 pixels.

View: *gs.statcounter.com/screen-resolution-stats/desktop/north-america.*

## Typography

A typeface contributes to a corporate identity. In most cases use a web safe font, see:

fonts.google.com/knowledge/glossary/system_font_web_safe_font.

You can also use Google fonts, see: *fonts.google.com*.
Here you will find many more and various fonts.

The Google fonts chapter explains how to apply this.

## Colors

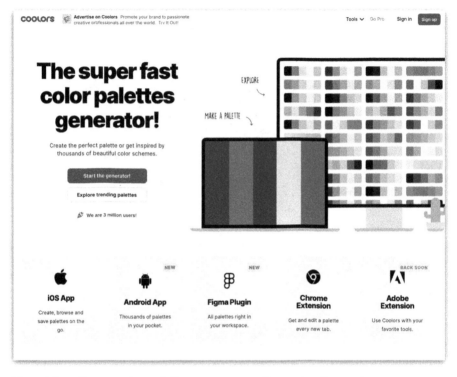

To put together a color palette you can use the web-site *coolors.co*. From the site you can use a color generator, diagrams or upload an image to put together a color palette.

The end result can be exported as an image including color code.

Tip: Make sure you use contrast. Text must be readable. Place a light text color on a dark background, or vice versa.

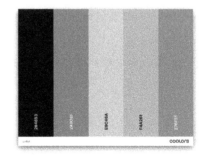

## Theme design

Having gathered information and gotten an idea of what structure you want to use, first make an outline of various pages and patterns.

# CREATING BLOCK THEME

In this book, we start with a basic block theme and expand it to a comprehensive block theme. I recommend following all the steps described in this book. In addition, I recommend using the same templates and files.

You can download all theme files:

> You do need a password:
> **Address: wp-books.com/block-theme/**
> **Password: carpediem_blocktheme**

While creating a block theme, you also work with code. It is recommended that you use a Code Editor. There are several Open Source Code Editors available. This book uses **Atom**. For more information see: *https://atom.io*.

The site editor is made to customize themes and you can also create block themes with it. The end result can be exported and used on other WordPress sites.

> **Note!** After adjusting files and styles manually, it is advisable to first clear the browser's cache and then refresh the website several times.
>
> If no style is applied, there may be something wrong with the code.
> Fix the code (go back one step) and try again.

Clear the browser cache after making
changes in the dashboard. You can
view the page by clicking the **View
Page** icon.

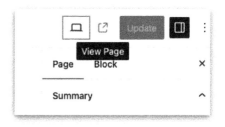

First create some pages and posts and then place a navigation menu in the
theme. This will help you get a better look at the website.

Here is an overview of the steps we will go through:

### 1. Basic block theme
This chapter manually creates a basic theme that is then customized using
the editor.

### 2. Style Basic block theme
This chapter defines the general style of the theme, such as dimensions,
colors and fonts.

### 3. Expand block theme
This chapter extends the basic theme with additional templates.

### 4. Add functions in block theme
This chapter adds additional features such as adding JavaScript, Google
fonts and more.

### 5. Block theme - Patterns
This chapter expands on the theme with patterns made in the style of the
theme.

## 6. Style variations

This chapter provides the theme with different style variations. This gives a user the choice to use a different color scheme and font.

## 7. Block theme - animation

In this chapter, the theme is provided with animations.

## 8. Export block theme

This chapter exports the custom theme. Editor customizations are not saved in the source code, but after exporting, they can be found in the source code.

## 9. Starter block theme

This chapter explains what a starter theme is and how to use it for further development.

## 10. Block theme generator

This chapter explains what a block theme generator is and how to use it for further development.

## 11. Block based child theme plugin

This chapter uses the Create Block Theme plugin and how to use it for further development.

## 12. Editor plugins

This chapter explains which editor plugins are available to develop a theme.

## 13. Apply theme plugins practically

This chapter creates a theme using plugins.

## 14. Theme with required or recommended plugins

This chapter explains how to add required or recommended plugins to a theme.

In each chapter where a theme is created you will find a download address. You can view these files and use them for your own design.

# BASIC BLOCK THEME

To create a basic block theme you only need a few files.

A basic block theme consists of:

**Theme_folder:**
- **style.css**
- **screenshot.png**
- **functions.php**
- **theme.json**
- **parts** (folder)
  - **header.html**
  - **footer.html**
- **templates** (folder)
  - **index.html**
  - **single.html**
  - **page.html**

The name of a template file is fixed. With this, files are automatically recognized by WordPress.

Go through all the instructional steps to create a basic block theme.

You may also use the files you downloaded.

Copying and pasting is faster than retyping various scripts.

**wp-books.com/block-theme**

**Page 76 - blockthemebasic**

## Steps

1. **Install WordPress** using **Local** or at a **web host**.
2. Go to the WordPress **installation folder**.
3. Go to the folder **wp-content/themes**.
4. In it, place a folder named **blockthemebasic**.
5. Then place the following blank files:

   ‣ **screenshot.png**.

   ‣ **style.css**.

   ‣ **functions.php**.

   ‣ **theme.json**.

   ‣ Two folders, **templates** and **parts**.

6. In folder **templates** place **index.html**, **single.html** and **page.html**.
7. In folder **parts** place **header.html** and **footer.html**.
8. Then open all theme files and **add code**.
9. Then from the **dashboard**, **activate** the theme.

All files except **parts**, **templates** and **screenshot.png** are text files. You can create them using a code editor. Caution! Use the correct extensions **.php**, **.css**, **.html** and **.json** when saving.

To better view pages and posts, you may provide the theme with a navigation menu. This can be created using the editor.

Scripts are taken from: *https://developer.wordpress.org/themes/block-themes* and the default block theme Twenty Twenty-Two.

## screenshot.png

This is usually a representation of the theme.

The image can be seen from the Dashboard after a theme installation.

Name: **screenshot.png**.
Size: **300 x 225 pixels**.
File format: **png**.

## style.css

Open **style.css** and copy lines 1 through 23. The information below will be displayed at **Dashboard > Appearance > Themes**.

```
1   /*
2   Theme Name: Block Theme Basic
3   Author: WP Books
4   Author URI: https://www.wp-books.com
5   Theme URI: https://www.wp-books.com/block-theme/
6   Description:  Everything you need to know about block themes.
7   Tags: full, site, editing, blok, thema, maken
8   Text Domain: blockthemebasic
9   Requires at least: 6.0
10  Requires PHP: 7.4
11  Tested up to: 6.0
12  Version: 1.0.0
13
14  License: GNU General Public License v2 or later
15  License URI: http://www.gnu.org/licenses/gpl-2.0.html
16
17  All files, unless otherwise stated, are released under the GN
18  License version 2.0 (http://www.gnu.org/licenses/gpl-2.0.html
19
```

**Styles** are **not** included in **style.css** but in the files **theme.json**, **templates** and **parts**. Style rules in style.css override the style rules of theme.json and are not accessible from the site editor.

Theme Name:    Name of theme.
Author:        Creator's name.
Author URI:    Creator's URL.
Theme URI:     URL of the theme.
Description:   Description of theme.
Tags:          Theme keywords separated by commas.
Version:       Version number.

# functions.php

A block theme does not need functions.php. Nevertheless, it is convenient to make use of it. This makes it possible to use additional styles, javascript, patterns and functions.

```php
1   <?php
2
3   if ( ! function_exists( 'blockthemebasic_support' ) ) :
4     function blockthemebasic_support()  {
5
6       // Adding support for core block visual styles.
7       add_theme_support( 'wp-block-styles' );
8
9       // Enqueue editor styles.
10      add_editor_style( 'style.css' );
11    }
12    add_action( 'after_setup_theme', 'blockthemebasic_support' );
13  endif;
14
15  /**
16   * Enqueue scripts and styles.
17   */
18  function blockthemebasic_scripts() {
19    // Enqueue theme stylesheet.
20    wp_enqueue_style( 'blockthemebasic-style', get_template_directory_uri()
21  }
22
23  add_action( 'wp_enqueue_scripts', 'blockthemebasic_scripts' );
24
```

Open **functions.php** and copy lines 1 through 23 from the file.

## index.html

This file is the home page of the website. The template specifies which **template parts** and **theme blocks** are included in this file.

```
     index.html
1    <!-- wp:template-part {"slug":"header","theme":"blokthemabasic","tagName":"header"} /-->
2
3    <!-- wp:group
·    {"tagName":"main","align":"full","style":{"spacing":{"padding":{"top":"0px","right":"0px","bot
·    {"inherit":true}} -->
4    <main class="wp-block-group alignfull" style="padding-top:0px;padding-right:0px;padding-bottom
·    wp:query
·    {"queryId":0,"query":{"perPage":5,"pages":0,"offset":0,"postType":"post","order":"desc","order
·    exclude":[],"sticky":"","inherit":true},"displayLayout":{"type":"list"},"align":"full","layout
5    <div class="wp-block-query alignfull"><!-- wp:post-template -->
6    <!-- wp:post-title {"isLink":true,"fontSize":"large"} /-->
7
8    <!-- wp:post-featured-image {"isLink":true} /-->
9
10   <!-- wp:group {"layout":{"type":"flex","allowOrientation":false}} -->
11   <div class="wp-block-group"><!-- wp:post-author {"showAvatar":false} /-->
12
13   <!-- wp:post-date /-->
14
15   <!-- wp:post-terms {"term":"category"} /--></div>
16   <!-- /wp:group -->
17
18   <!-- wp:post-excerpt {"moreText":"Read more","showMoreOnNewLine":false} /-->
19   <!-- /wp:post-template -->
20
21   <!-- wp:spacer {"height":"40px"} -->
22   <div style="height:40px" aria-hidden="true" class="wp-block-spacer"></div>
23   <!-- /wp:spacer -->
```

Open **templates > index.html** and copy lines 1 through 33 from the file.

At the top is a reference to the **header**.
Below that are a number of **theme blocks**, including the most important block, namely the **Query** block, better known as *The Loop*.

This piece of code ensures that posts and pages are processed correctly.
At the very bottom is a reference to the **footer**.

Go to **Editor > Templates > Index** :

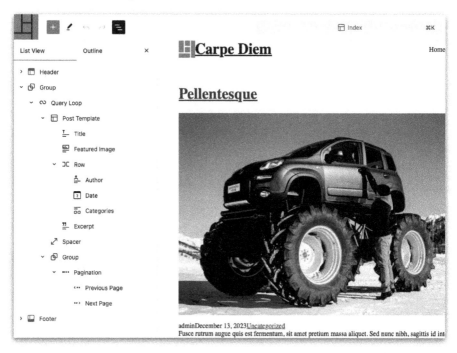

As you can see, this is not standard HTML. This code was created specifically for the site editor. After a template is loaded into a browser, standard HTML code is generated.

More info:

*https://developer.wordpress.org/themes/block-themes/templates-and-template-parts*

## single.html

This file ensures that an individual Post is fully displayed. This file is very similar to index.html, but supplemented with a response form. Open **templates > index.html** and copy lines 1 through 55 from the file.

```
                single.html
1   <!-- wp:template-part {"slug":"header","tagName":"header"} /-->
2
3   <!-- wp:group {"tagName":"main","align":"full","layout":{"inherit":true}} -->
4   <main class="wp-block-group alignfull"><!-- wp:post-title {"level":1,"fontSize":"large"} /-->
5
6   <!-- wp:post-featured-image /-->
7
8   <!-- wp:post-content {"align":"full","layout":{"inherit":true}} /-->
9
10  <!-- wp:spacer {"height":"40px"} -->
11  <div style="height:40px" aria-hidden="true" class="wp-block-spacer"></div>
12  <!-- /wp:spacer -->
13
14  <!-- wp:separator {"opacity":"css","className":"is-style-wide"} -->
15  <hr class="wp-block-separator has-css-opacity is-style-wide"/>
16  <!-- /wp:separator -->
17
18  <!-- wp:comments-query-loop -->
19  <div class="wp-block-comments-query-loop"><!-- wp:comments-title /-->
20
21  <!-- wp:comment-template -->
22  <!-- wp:columns -->
23  <div class="wp-block-columns"><!-- wp:column {"width":"40px"} -->
24  <div class="wp-block-column" style="flex-basis:40px"><!-- wp:avatar {"size":40,"style":{"border":{"ra
25  <!-- /wp:column -->
26
27  <!-- wp:column -->
28  <div class="wp-block-column"><!-- wp:comment-author-name /-->
29
30  <!-- wp:group {"style":{"spacing":{"margin":{"top":"0px","bottom":"0px"}}},"layout":{"type":"flex"}}
31  <div class="wp-block-group" style="margin-top:0px;margin-bottom:0px"><!-- wp:comment-date /-->
32
33  <!-- wp:comment-edit-link /--></div>
34  <!-- /wp:group -->
35
36  <!-- wp:comment-content /-->
37
38  <!-- wp:comment-reply-link /--></div>
39  <!-- /wp:column --></div>
40  <!-- /wp:columns -->
41  <!-- /wp:comment-template -->
42
```

At the top is a reference to the **header**.

Below that, a number of **theme blocks** have been added.

At the bottom is a reference to the **footer**.

Go to **Editor > Templates > Single Posts** :

The response form is automatically displayed, after a visitor calls up the full post.

This option can be turned off from **Dashboard > Settings > Discussion - Default post settings**.

## page.html

This file causes a Page to be displayed. In this case, it is a direct copy of single.html. Open **templates > index.html** and copy lines 1 through 55 into the file (or duplicate single.html).

At the top is a reference to the **header**.
Below that, a number of **theme blocks** have been added.
At the bottom is a reference to the **footer**.

Because it is a copy of single.html, the response form is included in it.
A visitor may also comment on a page in WordPress. To use this option, it must be activated from **Dashboard > Pages > page name**, see setting **Discussion**.

If you do not want to use a comment form, remove the lines
`<!-- wp:comments-query-loop -->` through
`<!-- /wp:comments-query-loop -->`, line 18 through 52.
Note, do not remove html tag `</main>`.

Below are the results.

```
                page.html
1   <!-- wp:template-part {"slug":"header","theme":"blokthemabasic","tagName

2
3   <!-- wp:group {"tagName":"main","align":"full","layout":{"inherit":true}
4   <main class="wp-block-group alignfull"><!-- wp:post-title {"level":1,"fo

5
6   <!-- wp:post-featured-image /-->

7
8   <!-- wp:post-content {"align":"full","layout":{"inherit":true}} /-->

9
10  <!-- wp:spacer {"height":"40px"} -->
11  <div style="height:40px" aria-hidden="true" class="wp-block-spacer"></di
12  <!-- /wp:spacer --></main>
```

Go to **Editor > Templates > Pagina's** :

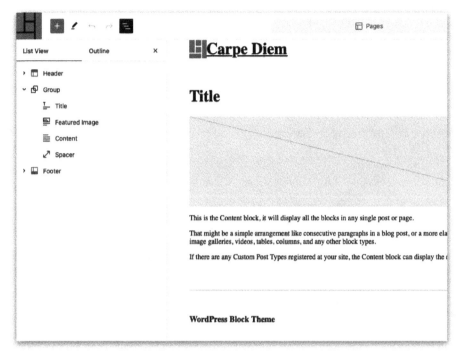

A page may be different in layout from a post.

In that case, you can change the structure and style.

## header.html

From the templates, references are included to a header and footer. These can be found in the **parts** folder.

Open **header.html** and place the code below. In the block **group** are a number of blocks such as **group**, **site-logo**, **site-title** and **navigation**. At the very bottom is a **spacer**.

```
                    header.html
1    <!-- wp:group {"align":"full","layout":{"inherit":true}} -->
2    <div class="wp-block-group alignfull">
3    <!-- wp:group {"layout":{"type":"flex","justifyContent":"space-between"}} -->
4    <div class="wp-block-group">
5      <!-- wp:group {"layout":{"type":"flex"}} -->
6      <div class="wp-block-group">
7        <!-- wp:site-logo {"width":40} /-->
8        <!-- wp:site-title {"fontSize":"large"} /-->
9      </div>
10     <!-- /wp:group -->
11
12     <!-- wp:navigation /-->
13   </div>
14   <!-- /wp:group -->
15   </div>
16   <!-- /wp:group -->
17
18   <!-- wp:spacer {"height":40} -->
19   <div style="height:40px" aria-hidden="true" class="wp-block-spacer"></div>
20   <!-- /wp:spacer -->
```

Go to **Editor > Patterns > Header** :

Include some pages in the **Navigation** block.

## footer.html

Open **footer.html** and insert the code below.

```
                footer.html        ●
1   <!-- wp:group {"align":"full","layout":{"inherit":true}} -->
2   <div class="wp-block-group alignfull"><!-- wp:separator {"opacity":"css","className":"is-style-wide"} -->
3   <hr class="wp-block-separator has-css-opacity is-style-wide"/>
4   <!-- /wp:separator -->
5
6   <!-- wp:spacer {"height":"25px"} -->
7   <div style="height:25px" aria-hidden="true" class="wp-block-spacer"></div>
8   <!-- /wp:spacer -->
9
10  <!-- wp:heading {"level":3} -->
11  <h3 id="footer-info">WordPress Blok Thema</h3>
12  <!-- /wp:heading --></div>
13  <!-- /wp:group -->
14
```

As you can see, the block **group** containing the block **separator**, **spacer** and **heading** is included.

Go to **Editor > Patterns > Footer** :

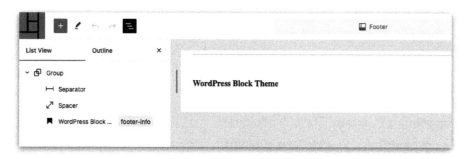

## theme.json

This file contains global styles, also known as global styles. Users can modify these styles using the editor. It is possible to include theme variations in one file, but it is better to divide them among several json files.

Configuration options:
▸ Enable or disable features such as initial, padding, margin and line height.
▸ Add color palettes, gradient and duotone.
▸ Add font sizes.
▸ Add default size for content and width.
▸ Add custom CSS.
▸ Assign parts to Templates.

Open the file and copy the code. As you can see, only a few styles are active, i.e., **spacing** and **layout**. The latter features a **contentSize** and **wideSize** of **840px** by **1100px**.

At **templateParts**, it is indicated that the theme uses a **header** and **footer**. These are references to the corresponding HTML files.

```
                    theme.json
 1   {
 2     "version": 2,
 3     "settings": {
 4       "appearanceTools": true,
 5       "color": {
 6         "palette": [
 7           {
 8             "slug": "",
 9             "color": "",
10             "name": ""
11           }
12         ],
13         "gradients": [
14           {
15             "slug": "",
16             "gradient": "",
17             "name": ""
18           }
19         ]
20       },
21       "spacing": {
22         "units": ["px", "em"]
23       },
24       "layout": {
25         "contentSize": "840px",
26         "wideSize": "1100px"
27       },
28       "typography": {
29         "fontFamilies": [
30           {
31             "name": "",
32             "slug": "",
33             "fontFamily": ""
34           }
35         ],
36         "fontSizes":[
37           {
38             "slug": "",
39             "size": "",
40             "name": ""
41           }
42         ]
43       },
```

theme.json information:
*https://developer.wordpress.org/themes/advanced-topics/theme-json*.

Global styles can be found in the site and page editor.

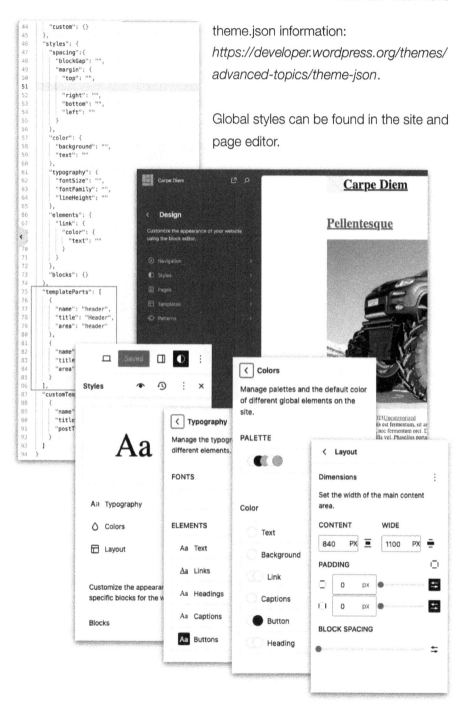

# STYLE BASIC BLOCK THEME

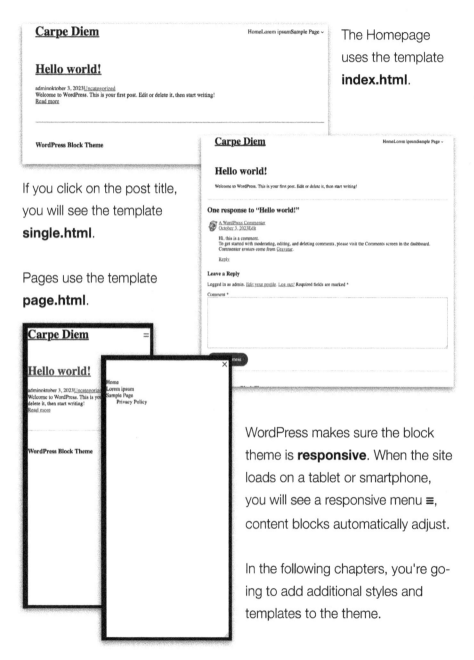

The Homepage uses the template **index.html**.

If you click on the post title, you will see the template **single.html**.

Pages use the template **page.html**.

WordPress makes sure the block theme is **responsive**. When the site loads on a tablet or smartphone, you will see a responsive menu ≡, content blocks automatically adjust.

In the following chapters, you're going to add additional styles and templates to the theme.

## Global styles

The theme could use some more formatting. Currently it using a style in which the **Content** and **WideSize** are defined. As we know by now, the global styles can be found in the **theme.json** file. Furthermore, a font, line spacing and base color are not used. Open the file and modify it.

You will see a version number, main categories and subcategories:

```
1   {
2       "version": 2,
3 >     "settings": {⊙},
46 >    "styles": {⊙},
74 >    "templateParts": [⊙],
86 >    "customTemplates": [⊙]
93  }
```

Under **settings** you will find:

```
3     "settings": {
4         "appearanceTools": true,
5 >       "color": {⊙},
21 >      "spacing": {⊙},
24 >      "layout": {⊙},
28 >      "typography": {⊙},
44        "custom": {}
45    },
```

Under **styles**:

```
46    "styles": {
47        "spacing":{
48            "blockGap": "",
49            "margin": {
50                "top": "",
51                "right": "",
52                "bottom": "",
53                "left": ""
54            }
55        },
56        "color": {
57            "background": "",
58            "text": ""
59        },
60        "typography": {
61            "fontSize": "",
62            "fontFamily": "",
63            "lineHeight": ""
64        },
65        "elements": {
66            "link": {
67                "color": {
68                    "text": ""
69                }
70            }
71        },
72        "blocks": {}
73    },
```

Under **templateParts**:

```
74    "templateParts": [
75        {
76            "name": "header",
77            "title": "Header",
78            "area": "header"
79        },
80        {
81            "name": "footer",
82            "title": "Footer",
83            "area": "footer"
84        }
85    ],
```

Under **customTemplates**:

```
86    "customTemplates": [
87        {
88            "name": "",
89            "title": "",
90            "postTypes": [ "post","page" ]
91        }
92    ]
```

**As you can see, all main and subcategories are opened and closed with curly braces { }. These, except the last one, are closed with a "," comma.**

With the code editor Atom, structure is made transparent. By clicking on the arrow **>** icon to the right of a line number, you can collapse and unfold nested code structure. To see vertical lines as shown in the example, go to *Preferences > Editor > Show Indent Guide*.

Use the styles below to add more formatting to the block theme. This will make the site more readable, thanks to a different font, appropriate line height and additional horizontal and vertical spaces around various blocks.

**Block spacing:**
**Line 48,** styles > spacing > blockGap -10px.

**Background color:**
**Line 57,** styles > color > background - #3e3e3e (dark gray).

**Text color, size, type and line height :**
**Line 58**, styles > color > text - #ffffff (white).
**Line 61**, styles > typography > fontSize - 16px.
**Line 62**, styles > typography > fontFamily - Sans-serif.
**Line 63**, styles > typography > lineHeight - 1.6.

View website.

| |
|---|
| **wp-books.com/block-theme**<br>**Page 94 - theme.json**  |

## Theme.json explained

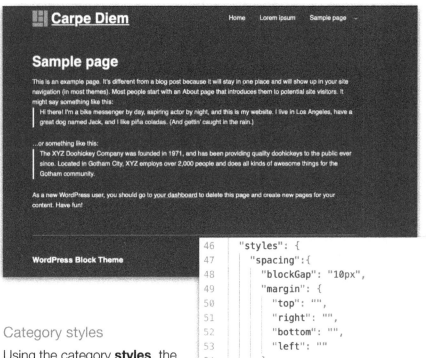

### Category styles

Using the category **styles**, the theme is provided with a default layout.

Styles are the default styles of a theme. Here you will find the categories **spacing**, **color**, **typography**, **elements** and **blocks**.

Blocks contains border and radius properties.

```
46    "styles": {
47      "spacing":{
48        "blockGap": "10px",
49        "margin": {
50          "top": "",
51          "right": "",
52          "bottom": "",
53          "left": ""
54        }
55      },
56      "color": {
57        "background": "#3e3e3e",
58        "text": "#fff"
59      },
60      "typography": {
61        "fontSize": "16px",
62        "fontFamily": "Sans-serif",
63        "lineHeight": "1.6"
64      },
65      "elements": {
66        "link": {
67          "color": {
68            "text": "#fff"
69          }
70        }
71      },
72      "blocks": {}
73    },
```

## Category settings

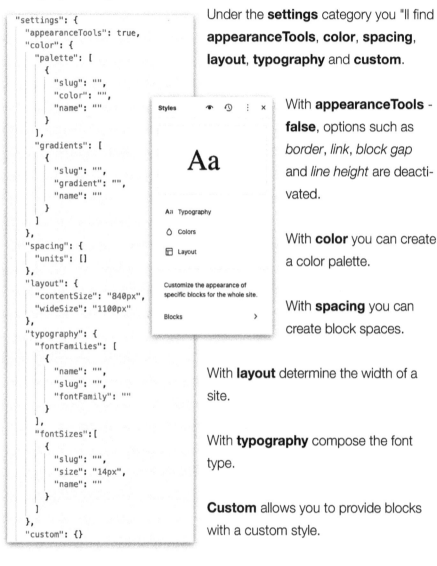

```
"settings": {
  "appearanceTools": true,
  "color": {
    "palette": [
      {
        "slug": "",
        "color": "",
        "name": ""
      }
    ],
    "gradients": [
      {
        "slug": "",
        "gradient": "",
        "name": ""
      }
    ]
  },
  "spacing": {
    "units": []
  },
  "layout": {
    "contentSize": "840px",
    "wideSize": "1100px"
  },
  "typography": {
    "fontFamilies": [
      {
        "name": "",
        "slug": "",
        "fontFamily": ""
      }
    ],
    "fontSizes":[
      {
        "slug": "",
        "size": "14px",
        "name": ""
      }
    ]
  },
  "custom": {}
```

Under the **settings** category you "ll find **appearanceTools**, **color**, **spacing**, **layout**, **typography** and **custom**.

With **appearanceTools - false**, options such as *border*, *link*, *block gap* and *line height* are deactivated.

With **color** you can create a color palette.

With **spacing** you can create block spaces.

With **layout** determine the width of a site.

With **typography** compose the font type.

**Custom** allows you to provide blocks with a custom style.

WordPress recommends including all style properties in the **settings** category. In the **styles** category, you use **variables** instead of direct values. The advantage of this method is that you only have to enter or modify a value once.

The example below includes style properties in the **settings - color** category.

```
 3    "settings": {
 4        "appearanceTools": true,
 5        "color": {
 6            "palette": [
 7                {
 8                    "slug": "foreground",
 9                    "color": "#ffffff",
10                    "name": "foreground"
11                },
```

The **styles** category uses **variables** instead of a fixed value.

A theme.json variable is constructed in the following way. The script begins with an announcement **variable ( )** with a reference to **WordPress settings** category **color** with **slug**.

A slug is a name selector and contains a color code or name.
The names (selectors) are separated by two dashes **--**.
Variables are used for color, typography and spacing, among other things.
In theme.json, this looks like this:

```
var(--wp--preset--color--foreground)
```

```
"styles": {
  "spacing":{∞},
  "color": {
    "background": "var(--wp--preset--color--background)",
    "text": "var(--wp--preset--color--foreground)"
  },
```

Styles

Colors

Manage palettes and the default color
of different global elements on the
site.

PALETTE

13 colors

Color

Text

Background

Link

After the file is saved, the styles can be seen in the site editor.

After a **color palette** has been created, it can also be used for **gradients**.
At **settings - gradients** you can enter the following:

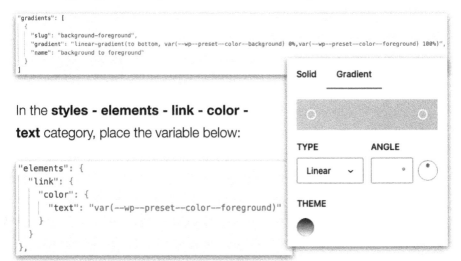

```
"gradients": [
    {
        "slug": "background-foreground",
        "gradient": "linear-gradient(to bottom, var(--wp--preset--color--background) 0%,var(--wp--preset--color--foreground) 100%)",
        "name": "background to foreground"
    }
]
```

In the **styles - elements - link - color - text** category, place the variable below:

```
"elements": {
    "link": {
        "color": {
            "text": "var(--wp--preset--color--foreground)"
        }
    }
},
```

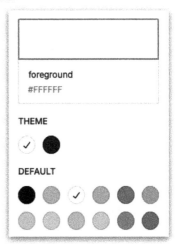

The advantage of working with variables is that you only have to adjust one color code. It is no longer necessary to place the color code under different categories.

More info: *developer.wordpress.org/block-editor/how-to-guides/themes/theme-json/*

You can download the custom file here.

> **wp-books.com/block-theme**
> **Page 98** - theme.json

## Expand theme.json

The json file of **blockthemebasic** has a number of categories and subcategories.
Theme.json of the **twentytwentytwo** theme contains more properties.

Go to the root folder of your WordPress installation: **name site > wp-content > themes > twentytwentytwo** and open the **theme.json** file.

The first thing to notice is that the order is different. A theme creator may decide this for himself.

```
 1   {
 2       "version": 2,
 3 >     "customTemplates": [▣],
34 >     "settings": {▣},
224 >    "styles": {▣},
351 >    "templateParts": [▣]
373  }
```

Under **settings > color** you can see duotone (line 37). This is an additional editor setting for images.

```
"color": {
  "duotone": [
    {
      "colors": [ "#000000", "#ffffff" ],
      "slug": "foreground-and-background",
      "name": "Foreground and background"
    },
```

Look at the build structure and place one **duotone** style in theme.json of **blockthemebasic**.

**Note!** all main and subcategories **except the last one** is closed with a "**,**" comma.

In theme.json from **twentytwentytwo** you will find under **settings > custom**: (line 140) **spacing**, **typography** and **line-height**. These are used for styling blocks. Take the category **settings > custom > typography** over in theme.json from **blockthemebasic**.

Note: do not adopt **spacing** and **line-height**.

```
"custom": {
  "spacing": {
    "small": "max(1.25rem, 5vw)",
    "medium": "clamp(2rem, 8vw, calc(4 * var(--wp--style--block-gap)))",
    "large": "clamp(4rem, 10vw, 8rem)",
    "outer": "var(--wp--custom--spacing--small, 1.25rem)"
  },
  "typography": {
    "font-size": {
      "huge": "clamp(2.25rem, 4vw, 2.75rem)",
      "gigantic": "clamp(2.75rem, 6vw, 3.25rem)",
      "colossal": "clamp(3.25rem, 8vw, 6.25rem)"
    },
    "line-height": {
      "tiny": 1.15,
      "small": 1.2,
      "medium": 1.4,
      "normal": 1.6
    }
  }
},
```

Then under **settings > styles > elements** for the elements **h1** and **h2** you are going to apply styles. The variable contains the **slugs**.

```
224  "styles": {
225 >   "blocks": {⬤},
281 >   "color": {⬤},
285    "elements": {
286      "h1": {
287        "typography": {
288          "fontFamily": "var(--wp--preset--font-family--source-serif-pro)",
289          "fontWeight": "300",
290          "lineHeight": "var(--wp--custom--typography--line-height--tiny)",
291          "fontSize": "var(--wp--custom--typography--font-size--colossal)"
292        }
293      },
```

These properties are used for styling headings.

Under **settings > spacing > units** (line 160) of theme.json of **twentytwentytwo** uses various units of measurement. This allows a user to choose a unit of measurement from within the editor.

Copy all measurement units into the json file of **blockthemebasic**.

```
"spacing": {
  "units": [
    "%",
    "px",
    "em",
    "rem",
    "vh",
    "vw"
  ]
},
```

From theme.json (line 171) it is also possible to enable or disable certain functions. With s**ettings > typography > dropcap - true** or **false**, the function **initial** can be used.

```
"settings": {
  "appearanceTools": true,
  "color": {▪},
  "custom": {▪},
  "spacing": {▪},
  "typography": {
    "dropCap": false,
    "fontFamilies": [▪],
    "fontSizes": [▪]
  },
```

L orem ipsum dolor sit ita separantur, ut disi perversius. Hoc sic ex vultum tibi, si incessum fing similis; Cur igitur, cum de re Duo Reges: constructio inter

Under **styles > blocks** (line 225) you can provide specific blocks with a global style.

```
"styles": {
  "blocks": {
    "core/button": {
      "border": {
        "radius": "0"
      },
      "color": {
        "background": "var(--wp--preset--color--primary)",
        "text": "var(--wp--preset--color--background)"
      },
      "typography": {
        "fontSize": "var(--wp--preset--font-size--medium)"
      }
    },
```

A selector you can use for blocks: "`core/name_blok`".

Each block has a specific name.

Copy the selector "`core/button`" including styles and paste it into **styles > blocks** of the json file of **blockthemebasic**.

The category **blocks** is already there. Adjust the variables, the background color will be **"foreground"** (white), the text color **"background"** (gray).

To see the additional adjustments, first place some **buttons**, **paragraphs** and **heading** blocks in a page.

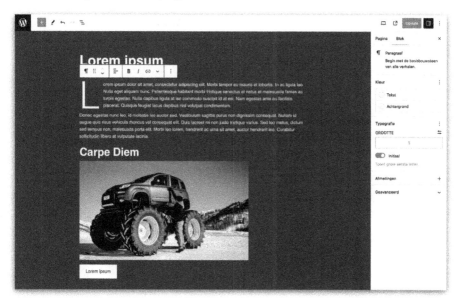

Taking a look at theme.json files from other block themes will give you more insight into structure and styling. More info: developer.wordpress.org/block-editor/how-to-guides/themes/theme-json.

You can also download the custom json file.

> **wp-books.com/block-theme**
> **Page 102 - theme.json**

## Category templatesParts

The categories **templateParts** and **customTemplates** indicate, among other things, which html files the theme consists of.

The **category name** indicates in which folder it can be found. The item "**name**" is the name of the html file. With "**title**" you give the component a name. With "**area**" the template location is indicated.

```
74    "templateParts": [
75        {
76            "name": "header",
77            "title": "Header",
78            "area": "header"
79        },
80        {
81            "name": "footer",
82            "title": "Footer",
83            "area": "footer"
84        }
85    ],
```

**blockthemebasic** (left) uses two templateParts files, header and footer.

```
"templateParts": [
    {
        "name": "header",
        "title": "Header",
        "area": "header"
    },
    {
        "name": "header-large-dark",
        "title": "Header (Dark, large)",
        "area": "header"
    },
    {
        "name": "header-small-dark",
        "title": "Header (Dark, small)",
        "area": "header"
    },
    {
        "name": "footer",
        "title": "Footer",
        "area": "footer"
    }
]
```

The **twentytwentytwo** theme (right) uses three headers and one footer. So it is possible to make use of various template-Parts.

The theme creator has already included a number of examples in various templates.

The site editor allows a user to compose or modify templates. You may choose the name of templateParts files.

## Category Custom Templates

A theme creator can provide a theme with Custom Templates.
This is a web page that is different from a standard page. Here you can
think of a page **Full Width**, **With Sidebar** or **Homepage**.

Several custom templates can also include a different Header or Footer.
These files (parts) must then be included in the theme.

In the Add Template section, an additional template is created from the site
editor by a user.

In this case, a Custom template is
created by a theme creator.

After this is added in the **templates**
folder, you may edit the file in **the-
me.json**.

```
"customTemplates": [
  {
    "name": "",
    "title": "",
    "postTypes": [ "post","page" ]
  }
]
```

In the category **customTemplates** you specify the **name** and **title** to be
used. Again, you may define the name yourself. **PostTypes** indicates whe-
ther the custom template is available for a page, post or both.

## Style responsive menu

After loading the theme into a tablet or smart-phone, a menu ≡ icon is visible. When you click on the icon, a white background color appears.

To change the background color, you can do the following: From the site editor, **select** the **Navigation** block.

From **Block Settings**, go to **Styles > Color**. At **Background**, select the same color as the background color of the theme, gray **#3e3e3e**.

At **Sub-menu & overlay text** select the color **white**.

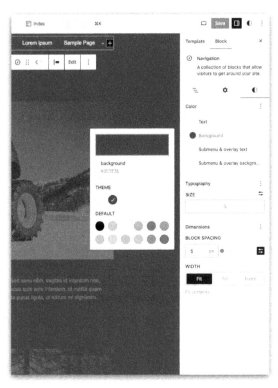

For more block spacing in the navigation menu, go to **Dimensions - Block Spacing** and use a value of e.g. **5px**.

After that, click **Save**.

# EXTEND BLOCK THEME

In the **Twenty Twenty-Two** theme, there are additional files and folders to be found. Folders such as **assets**, **inc** and **styles** have been added with associated files.

The **templates** folder contains additional templates such as **search**, **404**, **archive**, **blank** and **home.html**. These templates are created to generate specific content. Each template has a specific name indicating what it is used for. If a specific template is not present, the **index.html** template is used. The names of the templates are set by WordPress.

Files with a name such as **page-large-header.html** are custom templates. You may come up with your own name for these templates.

WordPress uses a template hierarchy. This specifies which templates you can use within the theme system. This applies to both classic and block themes.

The extension of classic template files ends with **.php** for block themes this is **.html**.

For more information about template files go to: *wphierarchy.com*.

## Template hierarchy

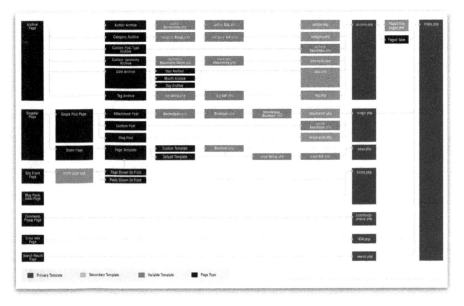

*wphierarchy.com.*

## Overview of templates you can use:

| Template | Beschrijving |
| --- | --- |
| index.html | Displays posts. |
| home.html | Displays posts on the home page or page after a static home page is selected. |
| front-page.html | Displays a home page. |
| singular.html | Displays an entire post or page. |
| single.html | Displays an entire post or page. |
| page.html | Displays a page. |
| archive.html | Displays categories, tags and archives. |
| author.html | Displays an author's latest posts. |

| Template | Beschrijving |
|---|---|
| category.html | Displays the latest posts of a category. |
| taxonomy.html | Displays the latest posts of a custom post type. |
| date.html | Displays posts from a specific date. |
| tag.html | Displays the latest posts of a tag. |
| media.html | Displays media items or attachments. |
| search.html | Displays search results. |
| privacy-policy.html | Displays a privacy policy page. |
| 404.html | Displays a message if no content is found. |

## Adding additional templates

In the **blockthemebasic** theme, three templates are available for the content generation namely **index**-, **single**- and **page.html**.
We will expand this theme with additional templates, **404**-, **archive**-, **search**- and **privacy-policy.html**.

**Steps**:

1. Go to the **WordPress installation folder > wp-content > themes > blockthemebasic > templates**.
2. Make four copies of **page.html**.
3. Rename this to **404**-, **search**-, **archive**- and **privacy-policy.html**.
4. Go to **Dashboard > Appearance > Editor > Templates** and edit the templates.

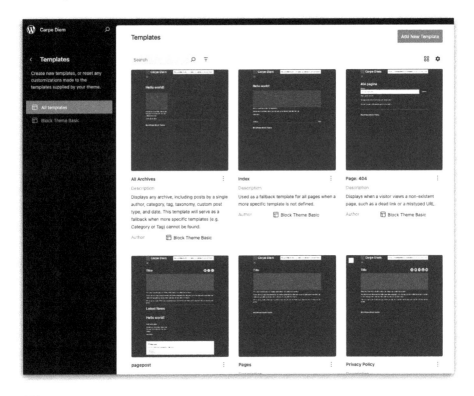

## 404- and search.html

A 404 template is applied after a page is not found.

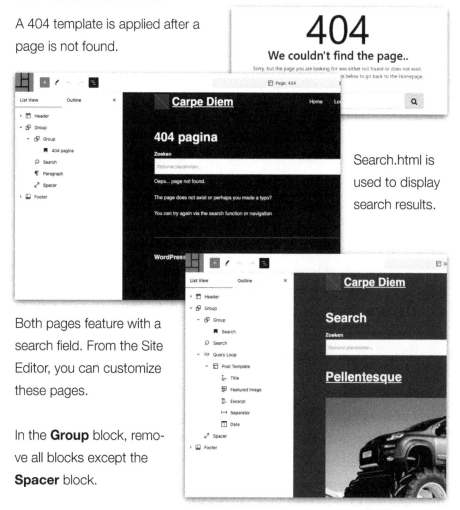

Search.html is used to display search results.

Both pages feature with a search field. From the Site Editor, you can customize these pages.

In the **Group** block, remove all blocks except the **Spacer** block.

**404**: Place the **Header**, **Search Field** and **Paragraph** blocks.

**Search**: Place the blocks **Header**, **Search field** and **Query loop**.
Block Setting **Query loop** - Activate, **Inherit query from template**.

Then click the **Save** button.

## Archive.html

An archive template displays the latest posts of a category. This is done after choosing a category from a link or categories list (using the categories block). Of course, the intention is to link a post to a category. By default, it is linked to the **Uncategorized** category.

**Create two additional posts** before customizing the template.

Open the **All Archives** template from the site editor. Not all templates update automatically. In this case, the entire formatting of page.html is adopted. Click **List View** for the structure layout.

### Customize Template

1. Remove all blocks in the **Group** block.
2. In the **Group** block, place the **Query loop** block.
3. Choose a default **pattern** - 3 columns.
4. Due to alignment, move the contents of the Nested Group to the main Group.
5. Delete the Nested Group block.
6. Place at the bottom of the link text **Read more...** .
7. Then click on the **Save** button.

If you want to provide the template with the **Featured image** block, you can add it under the **Title** block.

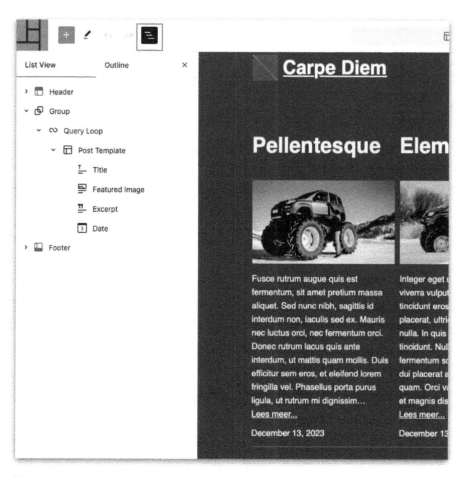

View site.

From the home page, click on a category link to see the page.

## Privacy-policy.html

The **Privacy Policy** template displays a page containing the privacy
policy. The template is applied when
the **URL slug** of a **page** contains the
name **privacy-policy**. The title of the
page may differ from the URL slug.

A default WordPress installation usually includes a privacy-policy
page. If it does not, you can create a new page.

**Open** the **Privacy Policy** template from the site editor.
As you can see, all the formatting has been taken from page.html.

To make sure the template is applied, an extra block is placed below the
title.

1. Select the **Title block**.
2. Below that, place the **Social icons** block.
3. Above the title, place the **Columns 50/50** block.
4. Drag the **title** in the left part, the **social icons** block in the right part.
5. Then adjust some block properties regarding alignment.
6. Click on the **Save** button.

View site.

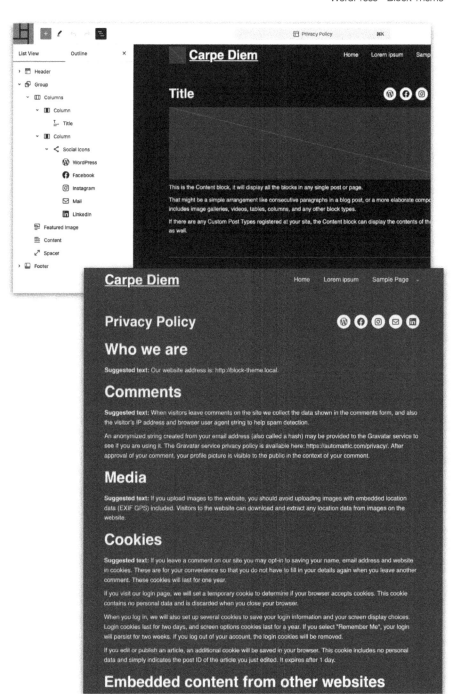

## Add custom template

In this chapter, you are going to provide the theme with a custom template. You don't have to type in the code for this yourself.

You have already created a custom template using the site editor, see the Add Template chapter. In this chapter, you will create a custom template manually. You can also download and view the files.

---

**wp-books.com/block-theme**
**Page 117 - custom_template**

---

**Steps**:

1. Make a copy of **page.html**.
2. Rename this to **pagepost.html**.
3. Open **theme.json**.
4. At **customTemplates**, copy the data (see image to the right).

```
"customTemplates": [
  {
    "name": "pagepost",
    "title": "Page and Post",
    "postTypes": [ "post","page" ]
  }
]
```

5. Go to the site editor and edit the custom template **pagepost.html**.

As the name of the file indicates, the template is used to provide a **page** with a number of recent **posts**.

After the template is opened, you're going to customize some of its components.

Use **List View**. This will show you the structure structure and blocks. Add Block **Columns 70/30**. Place the **Title** in the left column and the **Social icons** block in the right column.

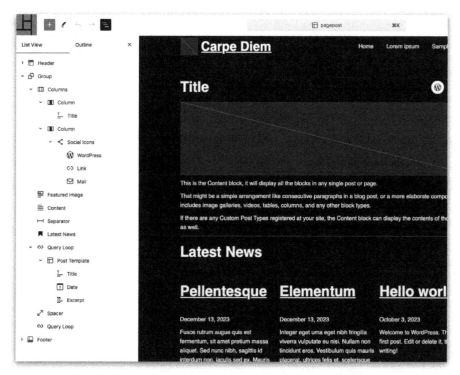

Under the **Post content** block you place a number of blocks:
**Separator**, **Header** and **Query loop**.

While placing the **Query loop** block, you can choose **Patterns > Posts > Grid**, a pattern with three posts next to each other.

Under the **Excerpt** block, place the link text **Read more...** .

If you want to provide the template with the **featured image** block, you can add it under the title block.

Then click the **Save** button.

The modifications are not saved in the **pagepost.html** file but in a temporary storage. This makes it possible to reset a page. After a reset, you always get the original structure.

By **exporting** the theme, modifications can be found in html files. Since the theme is not quite ready yet, we will perform this later.

## Apply Custom Template

Go to **Dashboard > Pages > New Page**. Give your page a **title** and **content**. Under Page **settings**, choose **template > Swap template** en select the template **pagepost**.

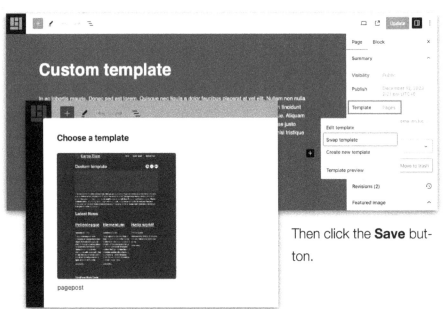

Then click the **Save** button.

Include the page in the **navigation menu** and view the website.

## Carpe Diem

Home    Lorem ipsum    Sample Page

## Custom template

In ac lobortis mauris. Donec sed est lorem. Quisque nec ligula a dolor faucibus placerat at vel elit. Nullam non nulla cursus, eleifend dui ac, volutpat libero. Suspendisse vel tincidunt est. Sed eget lacus massa. Vestibulum tincidunt porttitor fermentum. In sit amet odio fringilla, sagittis nunc ut, suscipit risus. Praesent eget faucibus augue. Aliquam vestibulum tellus nec blandit gravida. Integer vestibulum turpis vel rutrum ornare. Nulla sit amet arcu vitae justo rhoncus semper. Donec malesuada felis sed eros rutrum placerat. Donec at lacinia lorem. Curabitur id nisi tristique tellus pulvinar varius in eu sapien.

## Latest News

### Pellentesque

december 13, 2023

Fusce rutrum augue quis est fermentum, sit amet pretium massa aliquet. Sed nunc nibh, sagittis id interdum non, iaculis sed ex. Mauris nec luctus orci, nec fermentum orci. Donec rutrum lacus quis ante interdum, ut mattis quam mollis. Duis efficitur sem eros, et eleifend lorem fringilla vel. Phasellus porta purus ligula, ut rutrum mi dignissim...

Lees meer...

### Elementum

december 13, 2023

Integer eget urna eget nibh fringilla viverra vulputate eu nisi. Nullam non tincidunt eros. Vestibulum quis mauris placerat, ultrices felis et, scelerisque nulla. In quis orci in dui elementum tincidunt. Nulla quis tincidunt lorem. In fermentum sodales odio, a fermentum dui placerat ac. Donec vel augue quam. Orci varius natoque penatibus et magnis dis parturient...

Lees meer...

### Hello world!

oktober 3, 2023

Welcome to WordPress. This is your first post. Edit or delete it, then start writing!

Lees meer...

**WordPress Block Theme**

# FUNCTIONS IN BLOCK THEME

Adding features to a theme can be done using plugins. To avoid burdening a user with these, it is convenient to integrate them into the theme. This makes it possible to add tracking ID, exotic fonts or another responsive menu to a theme, among other things.

Adding features may seem like a complicated process, but it boils down to adding code to a theme. Many of these codes are available and can be found on the Internet. Using the right keywords will quickly get you to the code you need. For example: WordPress + Block theme + functions.php + Google Analytics code. Keywords in English usually give more results.

The file where you can add code is **functions.php**. This file is an integral part of both classic and block themes. A user can still install plugins if needed.

A common addition is to include JavaScript in a website. This allows the theme to include Google Analytics tracking code, for example.

The script is included in functions.php. The end result is that the tracking ID code is generated in the header or footer of the website.

You can also download the custom file.

> **wp-books.com/block-theme**
> **Page 122 - functions**.

## Google analytics code

After signing up with Google, you have access to a **tracking ID code**.

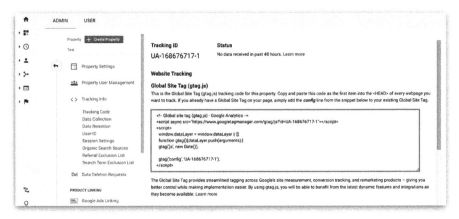

As stated, the **Global Site Tag** (gtag.js) with Trackings ID may be included in the **<HEAD>** tag of a web page.

Open the **functions.php** file.
Go to the last line, hit enter and add the code below.

```php
// Google analytics
<?php
add_action('wp_head','my_analytics');
function add_googleanalytics() { ?>
// Paste your Google Analytics code here
<?php }
?>
```

With **wp_head**, code is included in the head of a web page. For code in the footer use **wp_footer**.

Go to your Google screen and **copy** the entire script, **Global Site Tag**.

Go to **functions.php** and select:

`//Paste your Google Analytics code here.`

**Paste** the script.

```
24
25  // Google analytics
26  add_action('wp_head','my_analytics');
27  function my_analytics() {
28  ?>
29  <!-- Global site tag (gtag.js) - Google Analytics -->
30  <script async src="https://www.googletagmanager.com/gtag/js?id=AB-12345678-12"></script>
31  <script>
32    window.dataLayer = window.dataLayer || [];
33    function gtag(){dataLayer.push(arguments);}
34    gtag('js', new Date());
35    gtag('config', 'AB-12345678-12');
36  </script>
37  <?php
38  }
39
```

Above is the final result.

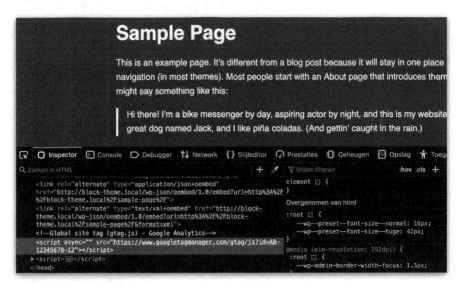

View site. On the screen, right-click and choose **Inspect**. As you can see, the Tracking ID code is included in the <head> tag.

## Google fonts

The **blockthemebasic** theme uses a **web safe font**. These are fonts such as Arial, Verdana, Helvetica, etc. In other words, fonts that can be found on any computer. This ensures that a website uses the correct font.

If you want to use an exotic font, use **Google Fonts**.
Go to **fonts.google.com** and select a font.
In this example, the font chosen is **Abril Fatface**.

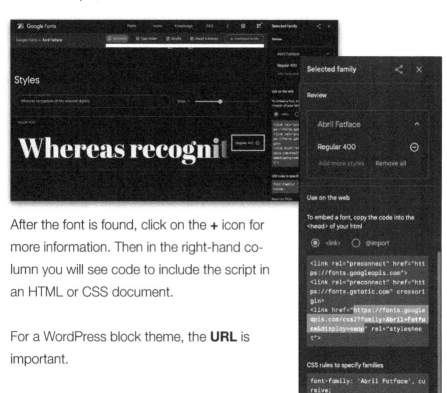

After the font is found, click on the **+** icon for more information. Then in the right-hand column you will see code to include the script in an HTML or CSS document.

For a WordPress block theme, the **URL** is important.

## Functions.php

Open **functions.php** and insert the code below.

```php
// Define fonts
function google_fonts() {
    wp_enqueue_style( 'google-fonts', 'fonts.google_url_here', false );
}
add_action( 'wp_enqueue_scripts', 'google_fonts' );
```

Go to **fonts.google.com** and **copy** the **URL** of the selected font:
https://fonts.googleapis.com/css2?family=Abril+Fatface&display=swap

Go to **functions.php**, select **fonts.google_url_here** and **paste** the URL.
The full code looks like this:

```php
// Define fonts
function google_fonts() {
    wp_enqueue_style( 'google-fonts', 'https://fonts.googleapis.com/css2?family=Abril+Fatface&display=swap', false );
}
add_action( 'wp_enqueue_scripts', 'google_fonts' );
```

A link to the Google font is included in the site.


The next step requires the **theme.json** file.

This specifies which elements and blocks use the font.

## Theme.json

Open the file **theme.json**.

Under **settings > typography** add a new **fontFamily**.

```json
"settings": {
  "appearanceTools": true,
  "color": {▣},
  "spacing": {▣},
  "layout": {▣},
  "typography": {
    "lineHeight": true,
    "fontFamilies": [{
        "fontFamily": "Sans-serif, Geneva",
        "name": "Sans-serif, Geneva",
        "slug": "sans-serif"
      },
      {
        "fontFamily": "Cambria, Georgia, serif",
        "name": "cambria-georgia",
        "slug": "cambria-georgia"
      },
      {
        "fontFamily": "\"Abril Fatface\", sans-serif",
        "name": "Abril Fatface",
        "slug": "abril-fatface"
      }
    ],
```

In **fontFamily**, a **Google font** is enclosed by a **backward** slash and **quote**: \"Abril Fatface\" .

Under **styles > elements - h1** to **h3**, add  **typography - fontFamily** and **fontSize**.

```
"styles": {
  "spacing": {⊟},
  "color": {⊟},
  "typography": {⊟},
  "elements": {
    "h1": {
      "typography": {
        "fontFamily": "var(--wp--preset--font-family--abril-fatface)",
        "fontSize": "var(--wp--custom--typography--font-size--colossal)"
      }
    },
    "h2": {
      "typography": {
        "fontFamily": "var(--wp--preset--font-family--abril-fatface)",
        "fontSize": "var(--wp--custom--typography--font-size--gigantic)"
      },
      "spacing": {
        "padding": {
          "top": "10px"
        }
      }
    },
    "h3": {
      "typography": {
        "fontFamily": "var(--wp--preset--font-family--abril-fatface)",
        "fontSize": "var(--wp--custom--typography--font-size--huge)"
      }
    },
    "link": {
      "color": {
        "text": "var(--wp--preset--color--wit)"
      }
    }
  },
```

At **fontFamily**, a slug indicates that the **Abril Fatface** font is used.

**FontSize** is already defined earlier under settings.

Under **styles > blocks - core/navigation**, add **typography and fontFami**ly.

```
"styles": {
  "spacing": {▪},
  "color": {▪},
  "typography": {▪},
  "elements": {▪},
  "blocks": {
    "core/button": {
      "border": {
        "radius": "0"
      },
      "color": {
        "background": "var(--wp--preset--color--wit)",
        "text": "var(--wp--preset--color--donkergrijs)"
      }
    },
    "core/navigation": {
      "typography": {
        "fontFamily": "var(--wp--preset--font-family--abril-fatface)"
      }
    }
  }
},
```

No **fontSize** is used under **typography**.

**Save** file and view site.

As you can see, the elements **H1** to **H3** and the block **navigation** use the Google Font **Abril Fatface**.

## Responsive Menu

A block theme is suitable for all screens. When the website is loaded on a narrower screen than the width of the theme, all blocks are displayed below each other.

The Block **Navigation** also adapts. A menu icon ≡ is displayed.

When the menu icon is clicked, all menu items become visible and the page behind the menu is hidden. From the site editor, you can customize a number of properties.

If you want a completely different layout and display, you can customize it with **functions.php**.

Before you start, create a submenu.

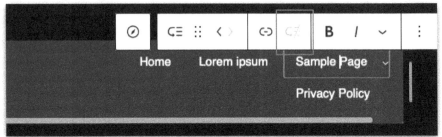

Select a **menu item**, see example. Click on the **Submenu** icon. Select e.g. the Privacy policy page.

You can also download the modified file.

> **wp-books.com/block-theme**
> **Page 132 - functions**.

## Step 1

From the site editor, click **Patterns > Header**.

After the Navigation block, add the **Custom HTML** block.

In the block, place the HTML code below:

```
<div class="burger">
  <div class="line1"></div>
  <div class="line2"></div>
  <div class="line3"></div>
</div>
```

This is for generating a hamburger menu.

You can now **save** the Template Part - Header.

Below is the result.

Then add additional features and CSS code.

## Step 2

Open the **functions.php** file and add the code below.

```php
// menu js function en script
add_action('wp_footer','my_menu');
function my_menu() {
?>

<script>
const navSlide = () => {
const burger = document.querySelector(".burger");
const nav = document.querySelector(".wp-block-navigation__container");
const navLinks = document.querySelectorAll(".wp-block-navigation__container a");

burger.addEventListener("click", () => {
  nav.classList.toggle("nav-active");

  navLinks.forEach((link, index) => {
    if (link.style.animation) {
      link.style.animation = "";
    } else {
      link.style.animation = `navLinkFade 0.5s ease forwards ${
        index / 7 + 0.5
      }s `;
    }
  });
  burger.classList.toggle("toggle");
});
//
};

navSlide();
</script>
<?php
}
```

The code consists of two parts. The first part is a function.

The second part is the script. This takes care of the operation of the menu and the **menu toggle**.

The script comes from:
*https://codepen.io/alvarotrigo/pen/KKQzbvJ* and was then modified.

## Step 3

Open the **style.css** file and add the code below.

```css
.wp-block-navigation__container {
    display: flex;
}
.wp-block-navigation__container a{
    display: block;


}
.wp-block-navigation:not(.has-background) .wp-block-navigation__submenu-container {
    color: #333;
}
.burger{
    display: none;
}
.burger div{
    width: 25px;
    height: 3px;
    background: #fff;
    margin: 5px;
    transition:all 0.5s ease;
}
@media only screen and (max-width: 760px){
    .wp-block-navigation__container{
        position: fixed;
        right: 0;
        top:0;
        height:100%;
        background: #333;
        display: flex;
        flex-direction: column;
        align-items: center;
        width: 100%;
        transform: translateX(100%);
        transition:All 0.5s ease-in;
    }
    .wp-block-navigation__container a{
        opacity: 0;
    }
    nav .wp-block-navigation__container{
        padding-top: 50px;
    }
    .wp-block-navigation__container button{
        opacity: 1;
    }
    .burger{
        display: block;
    }
}
.nav-active{
    transform: translateX(0);
}
@keyframes navLinkFade{
    from{
        opacity: 0;
        transform: translateX(50px);
    }
    to{
        opacity: 1;
        transform: translateX(0);
    }
}
.toggle .line1{
    transform: rotate(-45deg) translate(-5px,6px );
}
.toggle .line2{
    opacity: 0;
}
.toggle .line3{
    transform: rotate(45deg) translate(-5px,-6px );
}
```

Herein, the menu is provided with some additional features.

**Save** all files and view the site.

## Step 4

Go to the **site editor** to edit the header. **Select** the **Navigation** block.

Adopt the settings below to turn off the default toggle.

See **Block settings > Overlay menu - Off**.

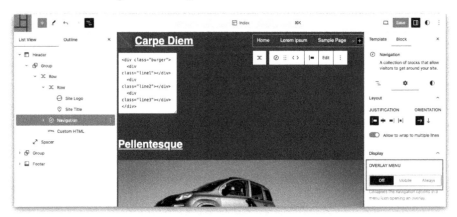

After that, click **Save**. To view responsive mode, you can use the Google **Chrome browser** for this purpose. After the site has loaded go to **Menu > View > Developer > Developer Tools**.

The **Toggle device toolbar**, phone/tablet icon button allows you to view the result (To be sure, make the menu text white).

If you want a different layout, Google "responsive menu."

There are many scripts and examples on the Internet.

To integrate a responsive menu into a block theme, it does come in handy to have knowledge of HTML and CSS. You can also use a responsive menu plugin.

# CREATE BLOCK PATTERN

A block theme defines the look and feel of a Web site. Among other things, it defines the dimensions, styling of blocks and color scheme. Most themes feature patterns. This complements a theme with various layouts. Patterns make a theme interesting, readable and contribute to its design.

After a pattern is inserted, a user does not need to lay out pages themselves. Sample text and images can be quickly and easily replaced without disturbing the layout.

Patterns consist of layout blocks created specifically for pages, posts and theme sections. These include page layouts, column layouts, call-to-action blocks, and various headers and footers.

In this chapter, you are going to add a pattern to the **block theme basic** theme. Before doing this, it is recommended that you first visualize a pattern first. Below you can see the design.

Cover block: background image, no content, full width, fixed background

Group

Columns (50/50), no width

Paragraph

Paragraph

## Block pattern in theme

As you see on the previous page, we are going to place a **Cover** block. Below that a **Group** with **Columns**. In both columns a **Paragraph**.

**Note!** Create the pattern in a **Page editor** (not a site editor).

The **Cover** block is **Full Width**. Under **Block options > Media settings**, select **Fixed background**. The **Minimum height of cover** is **295 px**.

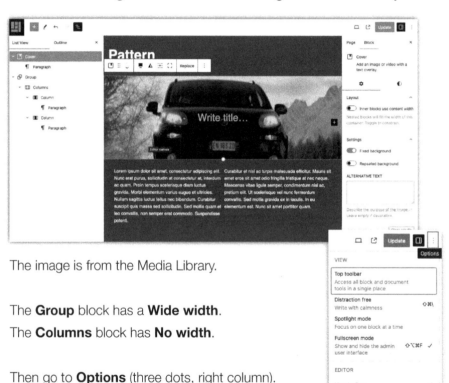

The image is from the Media Library.

The **Group** block has a **Wide width**.
The **Columns** block has **No width**.

Then go to **Options** (three dots, right column).
Click on **Code editor** and **copy** the code.

Open a Code Editor (Atom). Create a **new file** and **paste** the code.
Place a <?PHP ... ?> identifying code at the top.

```
 1   <?php
 2   /**
 3    * Title: Parallax block
 4    * Slug: blockthemebasic/parallaxblock
 5    * Block types: core/post-content
 6    * Categories: featured, text
 7    */
 8   ?>
 9
10   <!-- wp:cover {"url":"<?php echo esc_url( get_template_dire
  ·  panda.jpg","id":127,"hasParallax":true,"dimRatio":0,"minHei
11   <div class="wp-block-cover alignfull is-light has-parallax"
  ·  panda.jpg);min-height:295px"><span aria-hidden="true" class
  ·  container"><!-- wp:paragraph {"align":"center","placeholder
12   <p class="has-text-align-center has-large-font-size"></p>
13   <!-- /wp:paragraph --></div></div>
14   <!-- /wp:cover -->
15
16   <!-- wp:group {"align":"wide","backgroundColor":"gray","cla
17   <div class="wp-block-group alignwide eplus-G3scWo has-gray-
18   <div class="wp-block-columns eplus-xqjuA4"><!-- wp:column
19   <div class="wp-block-column eplus-a3GIv3"><!-- wp:paragraph
20   <p class="eplus-908vzX">Lorem ipsum dolor sit amet, consect
  ·  scelerisque diam luctus gravida. Morbi elementum varius aug
  ·  Sed mollis quam et leo convallis, non semper erat commodo.
21   <!-- /wp:paragraph --></div>
22   <!-- /wp:column -->
23
24   <!-- wp:column {"className":"eplus-FOek6S"} -->
25   <div class="wp-block-column eplus-FOek6S"><!-- wp:paragraph
26   <p class="eplus-VUJxzd">Curabitur et nisl ac turpis malesua
  ·  semper, condimentum nisl ac, pretium elit. Ut scelerisque v
  ·  quam.</p>
27   <!-- /wp:paragraph --></div>
28   <!-- /wp:column --></div>
29   <!-- /wp:columns --></div>
30   <!-- /wp:group -->
31
```

At **\*** *Categories*: is indicated under which category the pattern namely **featured** and **text**.

Save the file as **parallaxblock.php** and place the file in a new folder named **patterns** in the theme folder.

If you want to make the theme available to a wider audience, you can modify the PHP file. This is because the sample image comes from the media library. After a user has downloaded and installed the theme, they do not have the corresponding image. Therefore, it is recommended to include the image as part of the theme.

In the theme folder, place a folder named **assets**. In it you create a folder named **images**. In the images folder place the example image, for example panda.jpg.

Open the **parallaxblock.php** file. Modify lines 10 and 11.

```
10  <!-- wp:cover {"url":"http://blokthema-2.local/wp-content/uploads/2022/07/
    2121014271166.jpg","id":127,"hasParallax":true,"dimRatio":0,"minHeight":295,"minHeightUnit":"px"
    ,"isDark":false,"align":"full"} -->
11  <div class="wp-block-cover alignfull is-light has-parallax" style="background-image:url(http://
    blokthema-2.local/wp-content/uploads/2022/07/2121014271166.jpg);min-height:295px"><span aria-
    hidden="true" class="wp-block-cover__background has-background-dim-0 has-background-dim"></
    span><div class="wp-block-cover__inner-container"><!-- wp:paragraph
    {"align":"center","placeholder":"Titel schrijven...","fontSize":"large"} -->
12  <p class="has-text-align-center has-large-font-size"></p>
13  <!-- /wp:paragraph --></div></div>
14  <!-- /wp:cover -->
```

In it you will find a reference to a background image in the Media library.

Look for the **url** of an image, for example:

`http://blokthema-2.local/wp-content/uploads/2022/07/image.jpg`

Replace with:

```
<?php echo esc_url( get_template_directory_uri() ); ?>
/assets/images/panda.jpg
```

The php code `<?php echo esc_url` ... `?>` generates a url of the template directory followed by a forward slash **/** with a reference to the file.

**Save** the file.

Go to **Dashboard > Pages > New Page**.
See if the **Pattern** has become a part of the theme.

The pattern **Parallax block** can be found under the **Featured** and **Text** categories.

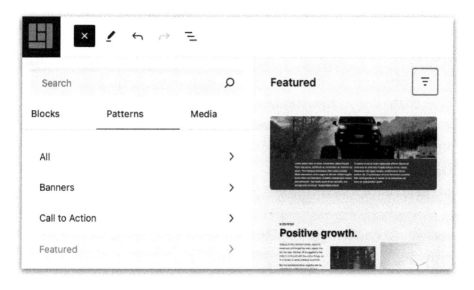

## Block pattern in theme.json

Block patterns can also be included in a theme using the **theme.json** file. There is no need to create a pattern yourself. In this case, we use a pattern from **wordpress.org/patterns**. Go to the website and select a pattern.

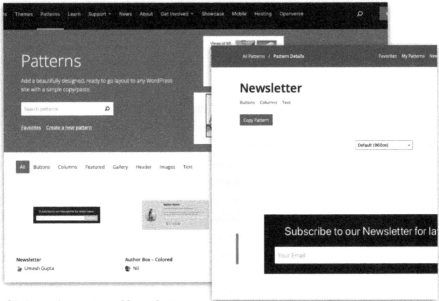

Click on the pattern **Newsletter**.

At the top of the screen, the **name** and **categories** (Buttons, Columns and Text) are displayed. In your browser's address bar, the full URL (slug) is displayed:

`https://wordpress.org/patterns/pattern/`**`newsletter`**`/`

Using the code below, you can create a reference to a pattern in word-press.org.

```
1  {
2     "version": 2,
3     "patterns": [
4       "Name Block Pattern", "slug-name-block-pattern"
5     ],
```

In the code, you can include the **name** and **slug name** of the pattern.

Open the **theme.json** file. Add the following code after **"version": 2,** .
Then adjust the two values. If you want more patterns, use a comma after
the first pattern.

Note! The last pattern is not ended with a comma. Below is the result:

```
"patterns": [
  "Newsletter", "newsletter",
  "Author Box - Colored", "author-box-colored"
],
```

Save the file. Block patterns can then be found under the **Text** and **Call to
Action** categories.

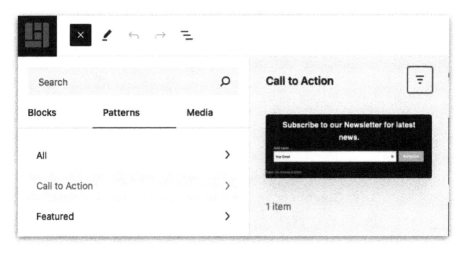

## Parallax scroll

While creating the block pattern **Parallax block**, in **Media settings** of the **cover** image block, a **Fixed background** was chosen.

This gives the background of a cover image a fixed position in the web page. To see the effect, it is important to include enough content in a page.

Create a new page with the title **Pattern**. In the page, place the following patterns: **Parallax block**, **Newsletter** and **Parallax block**.

Then replace the **cover images** and adjust the **background color** of the **Newsletter button**. After that, click the **Save** button.

Add the page to your navigation menu or view the preview. Use the scroll bar to see the effect.

If you want to learn more about page formatting and scroll effects, read the book **WordPress Gutenberg**. In it you will learn, among other things, how to use **anchors** to automatically scroll to different parts of a page.

## Remove block patterns

When creating a theme for a large audience, the corresponding block patterns are an important part of the whole.

With the right patterns, a user can easily create a page that matches the theme. After inserting a pattern, there is no need to change the style and formatting. The only thing that is modified is the content.

Default WordPress patterns often do not fit well with the theme. If the theme is intended for distribution, it is recommended to remove these patterns.

**Open** the **functions.php** file.
**Add** the **code** below and **save file**.

```php
// Remove standard patterns
function btb_theme_support() {
  remove_theme_support('core-block-patterns');
}
add_action('after_setup_theme' , 'btb_theme_support');
```

Go to **Dashboard > Pages > New Page** and view the remaining **Patterns**.

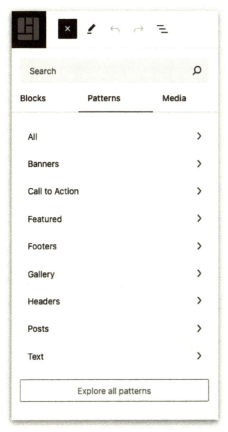

With core block patterns

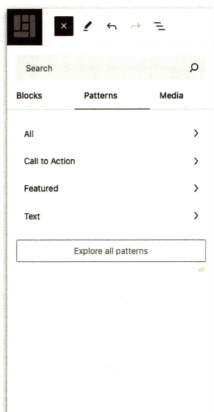

Without core block patterns

You can also download the custom theme.

wp-books.com/block-theme
Page148 - patterns

# STYLE VARIATION

Block themes can have one or more style variations. This makes it possible to choose from different styles within a single theme. This allows the font, color palette and blocks to change styles. The layout structure of the theme remains unchanged.

The *Twenty Twenty Two* theme features four style combinations. Variations can be found in **Dashboard > Appearance > Editor > Styles**. Select a different style combination.

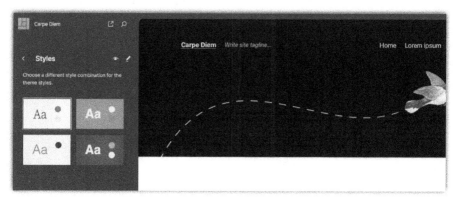

## Style variation in a theme

In this chapter, you are going to add a style variant to the *block theme basic* theme. This variant will contain the opposite color scheme. What is dark gray will become white and vice versa. This variant will also use a new Google font. You can also download the custom theme.

**wp-books.com/block-theme**

**Page 150 - variation**

Steps:

1. **Duplicate** theme.json.
2. Rename the duplicated file to **white.json**.
3. Place white.json in a new folder named **styles**.
4. **Open** the file **white.json** and edit it.
5. Add title, see example.

```
"version": 2,
"title":"White",
```

6. Under the category **typography -** *fontFamily*, *name* and *slug*.
   Replace **Abril Fatface** with **Lobster** (Slug is without capital).

```
{
  "fontFamily": "\"Lobster\", sans-serif",
  "name": "Lobster",
  "slug": "lobster"
}
```

7. Variable `--abril-fatface` replaced by `--lobster`.

```
"typography": {
  "fontFamily": "var(--wp--preset--font-family--lobster)"
}
```

8. Under the category **settings >
   palette** change the color code.
   `#ffffff` becomes `#3e3e3e`
   and vice versa.

9. **Save** file.

```
"palette": [
  {
    "slug": "foreground",
    "color": "#3e3e3e",
    "name": "foreground"
  },
  {
    "slug": "background",
    "color": "#ffffff",
    "name": "background"
  }
],
```

Because a **styles** folder with the file **white.json** has been added to the theme, a style combination is automatically recognized by WordPress.

The new font **Lobster** still needs to be logged in the functions.php file.

1. **Open** the **functions.php** file.
2. Copy the line `wp_enqueue_style( ... );`.
3. **Paste** it onto the next line.
4. Place a number (1 or 2) after `google-fonts`.
5. Then in the **URL** change the `font-name`.

```
// Define fonts
function google_fonts() {
    wp_enqueue_style( 'google-fonts1', 'https://fonts.googleapis.com/css2?family=Abril+Fatface&displa
    wp_enqueue_style( 'google-fonts2', 'https://fonts.googleapis.com/css2?family=Lobster&display=swap
}
add_action( 'wp_enqueue_scripts', 'google_fonts' );
```

**Save** file.

Then in the **stylesheet** replace color codes with variables.
This will also adjust the responsive menu after a style change.

1. Open **style.css**.
2. Replace color codes with variables.
#fff becomes `var(-wp-preset--color--foreground)`.
#eee becomes `var(-wp-preset--color--background)`.

```
.wp-block-navigation:not(.has-background) .wp-block-navigation__submenu-container {
  color: var(--wp--preset--color--foreground);
}
```

Go to **Dashboard > Appearance > Editor**. Click on **Styles**.

Select the style combination **White**.

Click **Save** (at the bottom) and view the website.

By using **variables** instead of color codes, you only have to adjust a color code once in this case. Of course, you can also apply this for a fontFamily and fontSize.

A user can modify the style variant by clicking **Edit Styles** (pencil icon).

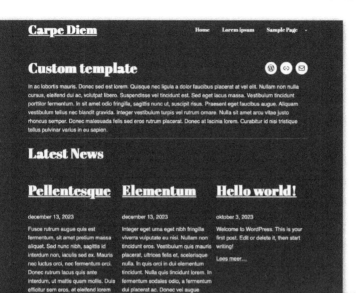

# ADD STYLE OPTIONS

From a **page editor** you work with standard block elements such as a paragraph, headline, list, quotes etc. If you want to make sure that these block elements match the theme, you can provide this with additional style options. This allows a user to decide which style is applied.

To see if the blocks fit the theme, you can do the following: create a new page and place text blocks. Then view the website to see which blocks can use additional style options.

As an example, we are going to expand the style options of the **Quote** block. After the block is included in a page, in the right column under Block **Settings > Styles**, you will see two styles namely **Default** and **Plain**.

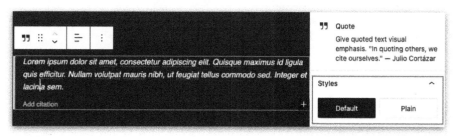

It is also possible to replace the default style with a new style. In this section, we are going to provide the block with an additional style option.

Tip: If the theme is created for a large group of users, it is recommended to replace the default option. After adding a block, the new style will be applied immediately.

You can also download the custom theme:

**wp-books.com/block-theme**
**Page 156 - style-options**

Before customizing the theme, it is useful to know what you are going to create. First, look at different CSS quotes. In this case, we are going to provide the block with a background color with rounded corners.

A "quote" symbol will be displayed before and after the quote.

## functions.php

Open the **functions.php** file and add the code below.

```php
// reference to quote stylesheet
add_action('init', function() {
  wp_enqueue_style( 'blockthemebasic-quote',
  get_template_directory_uri() . '/assets/css/btb-quote.css',
  array(),
  wp_get_theme()->get( 'Version' ) );
});

// reference to editor.js
function btb_gutenberg_scripts() {

  wp_enqueue_script(
    'btb-editor',
    get_stylesheet_directory_uri() . '/assets/js/editor.js',
    array( 'wp-blocks', 'wp-dom' ),
    filemtime( get_stylesheet_directory() . '/assets/js/editor.js' ),
    true
  );
}
add_action( 'enqueue_block_editor_assets', 'btb_gutenberg_scripts' );
```

The code includes a reference to a new **stylesheet**.

Below that is a reference to a **.js** file.

## editor.js

Open a code editor and create a new file.

Insert the code below and save the file as **editor.js**.

```
1  // adding block style
2  wp.blocks.registerBlockStyle(
3    'core/quote',
4    [{
5      name: 'btb-quote',
6      label: 'BTB Quote',
7    }]
8  );
```

Then place the file in the **assets > js** folder.

This file registers a new block style.


**name:'btb-quote'** selector name you can use in CSS.

**label:'BTB Quote'** name in the Editor under **Options > Styles**.


WordPress generates with this code a class name:

**.is-style-btb-quote**.


This is needed in the CSS file to give the new quote block the correct properties.

## Stylesheet

Create a new stylesheet named **btb-quote.css**. Add the code below. Place the file in the **assets > css** folder.

```
 1   /* BTB Quote */
 2   blockquote.wp-block-quote.is-style-btb-quote{
 3       font-size: 18px;
 4       font-style: italic;
 5       padding: 50px 60px 30px 55px;
 6       line-height:1.6;
 7       position: relative;
 8       border-left: 0;
 9       color: var(--wp--preset--color--background);
10       background-color: var(--wp--preset--color--foreground);
11       -webkit-border-radius: 25px;
12       -moz-border-radius: 25px;
13       border-radius: 25px;
14   }
15
16   blockquote.wp-block-quote.is-style-btb-quote::before{
17       content: "\201C";
18       font-size:4em;
19       position: absolute;
20       left: 20px;
21       top:0px;
22   }
23
24   blockquote.wp-block-quote.is-style-btb-quote::after{
25       content: "\201D";
26       font-size:4em;
27       position: absolute;
28       right: 40px;
29       bottom:-20px;
30   }
```

As you can see, the class **.is-style-btb-quote** has been added to the selectors. This applies the formatting only to a Quote block with the style **BTB Quote**. Note that a class name always starts with a '**.**' period.

## Apply Style

Open a new page and place three citation blocks.

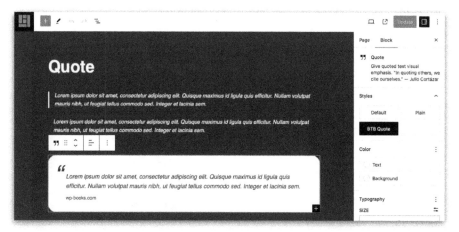

In the example, all style options are applied. In the last block with the style **BTB Quote**, the closing quote character is not shown in the editor, at the front end of the site it is shown.

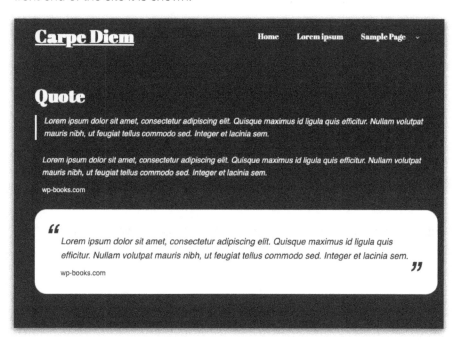

## Remove block style option

If you want to remove a default block option, you can modify the code in the **editor.js** file. Open the file and add additional code.

```
1   // block style options
2   wp.domReady(() => {
3   // remove block style
4     wp.blocks.unregisterBlockStyle(
5       'core/quote',
6       ['plain']
7     );
8   });
9
10  // adding block style
11  wp.blocks.registerBlockStyle(
12    'core/quote',
13    [{
14      name: 'btb-quote',
15      label: 'BTB Quote',
16    }]
17  );
```

Then **save** the file.

Look at the editor.

As you can see, the Style option **Plain** Formatting has been removed.

After inserting a new Quote block, the **Default** formatting is applied.

## Block style replacement

If the intention is to apply the BTB Quote style as a **Default** style, it is not necessary to perform all the operations described in the previous sections. In that case, you can include the CSS styles directly in the **style.css** file. Then replace the class name `.is-style-btb-quote` for `.is-style-default`.

```css
1  /* BTB Quote */
2  blockquote.wp-block-quote.is-style-btb-quote{
3      font-size: 18px;
4      font-style: italic;
5      padding: 50px 60px 30px 55px;
6      line-height:1.6;
7      position: relative;
8      border-left: 0;
9      color: var(--wp--preset--color--background);
10     background-color: var(--wp--preset--color--foreground);
11     -webkit-border-radius: 25px;
12     -moz-border-radius: 25px;
13     border-radius: 25px;
14 }
15
16 blockquote.wp-block-quote.is-style-btb-quote::before{
17     content: "\201C";
18     font-size:4em;
19     position: absolute;
20     left: 20px;
21     top:0px;
22 }
23
24 blockquote.wp-block-quote.is-style-btb-quote::after{
25     content: "\201D";
26     font-size:4em;
27     position: absolute;
28     right: 40px;
29     bottom:-20px;
30 }
```

## Core Blocks

When you are going to modify some block properties in the source code, it is good to know what block names are used. Due to translation, it is not easy to find out the original names. Below is a list of some Core blocks:

core/archives

core/audio

core/button

core/buttons

core/calendar

core/categories

core/code

core/column

core/columns

core/cover

core/file

core/latest-comments

core/latest-posts

core/legacy-widget

core/gallery

core/group

core/heading

core/image

core/list

core/media-text

core/more

core/navigation

core/navigation-link

core/nextpage

core/paragraph

core/preformatted

core/pullquote

core/quote

core/rss

core/search

core/separator

core/shortcode

core/social-link

core/social-links

core/spacer

core/subhead

core/table

core/tag-cloud

core/text-columns

core/verse

core/video

core/widget-area

## Classes

As you know by now, block elements and block styles have their own class name. You can use these to modify the formatting or to create a new style.

Example, Block **Quote**.
Block Core name: **core/quote**.
Block Class name: **wp-block-quote**.
Block Style - Default, Class name: **default**.
Block Style - Without formatting, Class name: **plain**.

After this block with a chosen style is included in a page, a class name is generated in the HTML code, for example:
class="wp-block-quote **is-style-default**"

To provide blocks with style properties, you can use three classes in this case:
.wp-blockquote (without style)
.is-style-**default** (default)
.is-style-**plain** (without formatting)

In the Block style replacement section, a number of classes have been applied.

If you want to know which class names are generated, you can do the following. In this example, the Quotation block is used.

Create a new page and place three Quote blocks in it.
Style options for the three blocks:
Block 1 - **no style**, Block 2 - **default** and Block 3 - **no formatting**.

Go to **Options** (3 dots) **> Code editor**.

As you can see in the HTML code, the attribute **class** shows which class name was generated.

A theme is more than just the shell of a Web site. By matching block elements to the theme, you create uniformity. These extra touches make a Web site fun and interesting. By using additional block styles, you provide diversity. This gives a user plenty of choices for composing pages and posts.

If you want style options for block elements, by now you know how to do this. As an additional exercise, you may create your own styles for the block **List**.

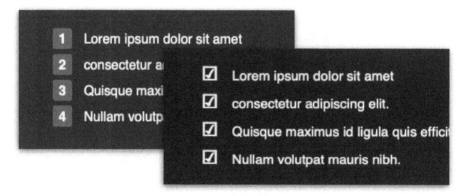

Note! A list is numbered `<ol>` or unnumbered `<ul>`. A lot of variation is possible. The sample file contains list styles.

If you are looking for the right CSS code, use a search engine. With the right keywords, you'll find quick results: list style CSS....
Or go to: *https://sharkcoder.com/blocks/list*.

Tip: If you create a theme with style options make sure they are also appropriate for style variations.

More information on HTML and CSS, visit: *https://www.w3schools.com*.

# BLOCK THEME ANIMATION

With a static theme, you can use color and format to clearly indicate which parts are important to a site visitor. With movement you can reinforce this effect. This gives a block element extra attention, making a visitor absorb information faster. A theme becomes dynamic and fun.

There are many types of effects possible, but be careful not to turn it into a carnival. Make sure an animation contributes to the structure and readability of a Web site.

Because the block theme is made up of HTML templates, it is fairly easy to add effects, including animation, to it.

Before implementing this, it is useful to know what effect you want to apply. This chapter will use two effects: Fade In and TypWriter effect. There are plenty of CSS examples on the Internet.

In this theme, templates are provided with a **Fade in** effect. This can be seen when a page or post is loaded. During loading the title appears using a **TypeWriter** effect.

You can also download the codes:

**wp-books.com/block-theme**
**Page 168 - animation**

```
/* Animatie Fade In */
.fade-in-text {
  animation: fadeIn 3s;
}

@keyframes fadeIn {
  0% {
    opacity: 0;
  }

  100% {
    opacity: 1;
  }
}

/* Animation TypeWriter - Note: title of
.anim-typewriter {

  overflow: hidden;
  animation: typing 4s steps(100, end);
  white-space: nowrap;
  box-sizing: border-box;
}

.anim-typewriter a {
  text-decoration: none;
}

@keyframes typing {
  from {
    width: 0%
  }

  to {
    width: 100%
  }
}
```

**Download** and open the file **animation.css**.

Included in the CSS code is a **Class** named `.fade-in-text`. Included in it is the animation **fadeIn** and duration.

At `@keyframes fadeIn` is specified with which transparency value it starts and ends.

Below that you will find the **Class** `.anim-typewriter`. This contains the animation **typeWriter** and duration included.

At `@keyframes typing` indicates with which width the text block begins and ends.

**Copy** the code.

Now go to the theme folder and paste this into the **style.css** file.

Then go to **Dashboard > Appearance > Editor**.
The **index page** will be displayed. Click on the page to edit it.

Use **List View** to see the structure layout.

From **List View**, select the block **Post template**.

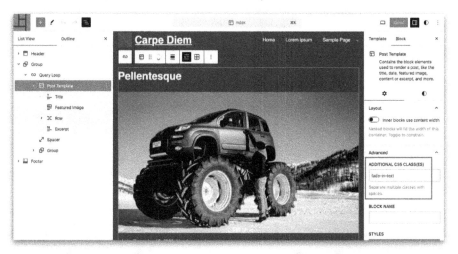

In the right column under **Block Settings** (cog icon) > **Advanced - EX-TRA CSS-CLASS(ES)** place the class name **fade-in-text**. Note that this text field uses a class name without a dot.

Then go back to **List View** and select the **Title** block.

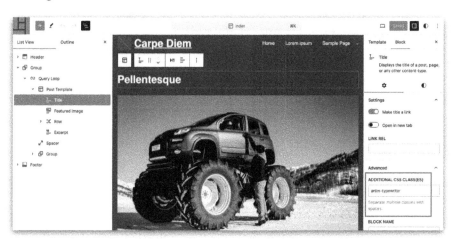

In the right column under **Block Settings > Advanced - EXTRA CSS-CLASS(ES)** place the class name **anim-typewriter**.

Click the **Save** button and view the website.

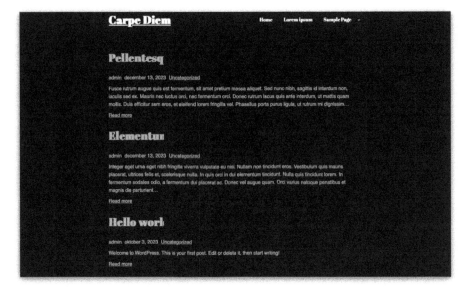

If you want the animations to be applied to other templates then you can repeat this process.

If a template is missing the **Post template** block then you can use the **Group** block for a **fade-in-text** effect.

Note! After entering the class name **anim-typewriter** the position of the **Title** block may change. If this happens you can place the **Title** block in a new **Columns** block.

On the next page you can see a screenshot of the template **Pages**. Using **List View** you can see the new structure.

Once all **Templates** have been adjusted, click the **Save** button and view the website.

# EXPORT BLOCK THEME

While developing a block theme, **structural** and **style** modifications from the site editor are not saved in the source code. Therefore, it is possible to reset a theme. Only after the theme has been exported, these changes do appear in the source code.

If you're done with the theme, then it's time to export it. Go to **Dashboard > Appearance > Editor**. The **index page** will be displayed. Click on the page to edit it. Go to **Options**, 3 dots at the top right and select **Export**.

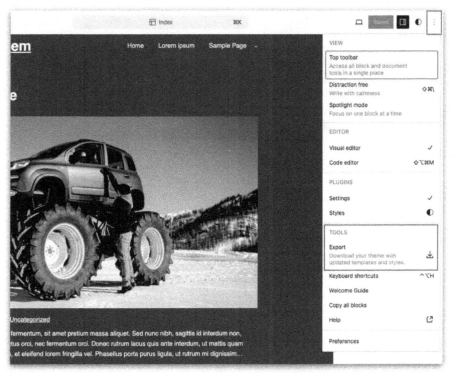

The theme can then be found as a **zip** file in a **download** folder.
A user can use this file to install and activate the theme.

If you want the theme to be included in the *WordPress.org/themes* theme library, it must first be submitted. Only after a thorough review and approval will the theme be released.

A requirement for submission is that a file named **readme.txt** is included in the theme's folder.

An example can be found in the Twenty Twenty Two theme.

```
=== Twenty Twenty-Two ===
Contributors: wordpressdotorg
Requires at least: 5.9
Tested up to: 6.0
Requires PHP: 5.6
Stable tag: 1.2
License: GPLv2 or later
License URI: http://www.gnu.org/licenses/gpl-2.0.html

== Description ==

Built on a solidly designed foundation, Twenty Twenty-Two embraces the idea that everyone
deserves a truly unique website. The theme's subtle styles are inspired by the diversity
and versatility of birds: its typography is lightweight yet strong, its color palette is
drawn from nature, and its layout elements sit gently on the page.

The true richness of Twenty Twenty-Two lies in its opportunity for customization. The theme
is built to take advantage of the Full Site Editing features introduced in WordPress 5.9,
which means that colors, typography, and the layout of every single page on your site can
be customized to suit your vision. It also includes dozens of block patterns, opening the
door to a wide range of professionally designed layouts in just a few clicks.

Whether you're building a single-page website, a blog, a business website, or a portfolio,
Twenty Twenty-Two will help you create a site that is uniquely yours.
```

Make sure the theme meets all the requirements and go through all the guidelines before uploading the theme.

Learn more:
*https://wordpress.org/themes/getting-started*.

Upload theme:
*https://wordpress.org/themes/upload*.

With the advent of the site editor and the ease of creating a block theme, many block themes will appear in the near future.

Currently, many WordPress sites still use classic themes. It will be some time before these are completely replaced.

You can also download the fully customized theme.

**wp-books.com/block-theme**
**Page 176 - blockthemebasic**

# REINVENT THE WHEEL?

By now, you know what steps to take to create a WordPress block theme. With this knowledge, it is even possible to modify existing block themes.

By downloading and studying block themes, you can see how theme creators have set this up. In some cases, it features JavaScript or an added Font. Other theme creators use SASS, a variant of CSS.

There are now many basic block themes available that are made specifically for setting up your own theme. WordPress calls these a **Base Theme** or a **Block Based Starter Theme**. A characteristic of a starter theme is that it contains a number of basic styles and features. The goal of a base theme is to develop it further into a full-fledged final product.

Working with a Base Theme is not immediately plug and play. It takes time to understand its structure, functions and styles.

WordPress also has a Base Theme called **Blockbase**. You can download it from: *https://wordpress.com/theme/blockbas*e or from **Dashboard > Appearance > Themes**.

The **Blockbase** theme has interesting components that you can integrate into your own website. There is no need to develop the theme further. You can also use some of its components.

**Install** and **Activate** the theme **Blockbase** by Automattic. Then go to **Dashboard > Appearance > Editor** and view the **index** page.

From the right column **Styles > Typography > Fonts** it is possible to choose from a large selection of fonts (first activate *Font family* using *typography options* - 3 dots).

If you want the same feature in your own theme, you can do the following. Go to the **Blockbase** theme folder and look at the folder structure.

As you can see, the **fonts** folder is found in the **inc** and **assets** folders.

Adding a function is done with **function.php**. From **theme.json** is indicated which fonts are used.

## Follow the path

---

**Create a new WordPress site.**

**Install** and **Activate** the **blockthemebasic theme - page 76.**

---

After looking at the Blockbase folder structure, it is broadly clear which folders you need for this. You can be more sure by following the path.

Go to the **Blockbase** theme folder and open the **functions.php** file.

```
 98
 99    require get_template_directory() . '/inc/fonts/custom-fonts.php';
100
```

As you can see, a reference is included to the folder:

**inc/fonts/custom-fonts.php**.

**Copy** this line and **paste** it into **functions.php** of your own theme.

Then **copy** the **inc folder** and **paste** it into your theme.

Then open the file **custom-fonts.php**.

```
21   function get_style_css( $slug ) {
22     $font_face_file = get_template_directory() . '/assets/fonts/' . $slug . '/font-face.css';
23     if ( ! file_exists( $font_face_file ) ) {
24       return '';
25     }
26     $contents = file_get_contents( $font_face_file );
27     return str_replace( 'src: url(./', 'src: url(' . get_template_directory_uri() . '/assets/fonts/' . $slug . '/',
 •     $contents );
28   }
```

This refers to a folder **assets/fonts**.

**Copy** the **fonts folder** and **paste** it into the assets folder of your own theme.

Open the **Blockbase** file **theme.json**.

```
344     "typography": {
345       "fontFamilies": [
346         {
347           "fontFamily": "-apple-system, BlinkMacSystemFont, 'Segoe UI',
348           "slug": "system-font",
349           "name": "System Font"
350         },
351         {
352           "fontFamily": "Arvo, serif",
353           "slug": "arvo",
354           "name": "Arvo",
355           "provider": "blockbase-fonts"
356         },
357         {
358           "fontFamily": "'Bodoni Moda', serif",
359           "slug": "bodoni-moda",
360           "name": "Bodoni Moda",
361           "provider": "blockbase-fonts"
362         },
363         {
364           "fontFamily": "Cabin, sans-serif",
365           "slug": "cabin",
366           "name": "Cabin",
367           "provider": "blockbase-fonts"
368         },
```

Starting on line 344 under **settings > typography**, the fontFamilies are included. **Copy** lines 344 through 542.

**Open** the **theme.json** file from the **blockthemebasic** theme. Select the **typography** category and **paste** the code.

Then you may delete the unnecessary files from the **assets** , **inc** and **customizer** folders.

Go to the site editor and edit the **index** page. Select the **Title** block.

From the right column **Styles > Typography** 3 dots > **Font family**, select font **Bodoni Mode**.

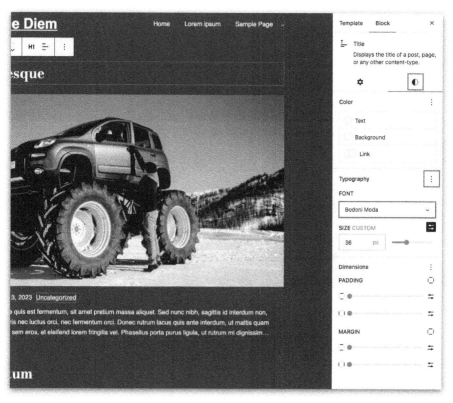

You can also download the custom theme.

wp-books.com/block-theme
Page 182 - blockthemebasic

# BLOCK THEME GENERATOR

The previous chapter described the possibility of starting with a starter theme. A starter theme generally has a certain style, structure and features. This can be an advantage or a disadvantage.

It is an advantage if the theme has the right components. If it does not, it takes extra time to remove and adjust it.

You can also use a **Block Theme Generator**. With this you generate a theme with minimal style or even no formatting. You get to decide which *custom templates*, *templates* and *parts* to start with.

A Generator Starter Theme contains only the necessary files. A web builder now only needs to add your own style and features.

Meanwhile, there are a number of block theme generators available that can help you.

## Themegen

Go to *www.themegen.app* and sign up. After a link is sent, you can use this generator to create code for theme.json.

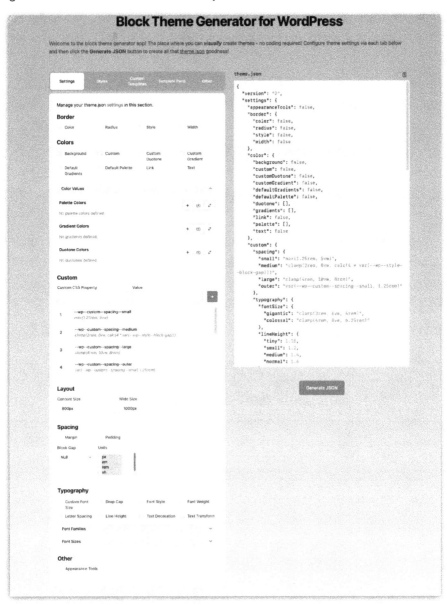

Using tabs, the categories of theme.json are made visually visible.
This makes it easy to add interpretation to the various components.

The code is generated only after clicking the **Generate JSON** button.
After that, you may copy and paste the code into your own theme.json file.

The other files such as style.css, functions.php, custom templates, templates and parts you can then manually add to the theme yourself.

You can also add the theme.json file to a theme generated by other Generators. These provide a complete starter theme, but do not use an interface like Themegen's.

# Full Site Editing - Block theme generator

Go to *www.fullsiteediting.com/block-theme-generator*.

Please use the form and select one of the starter themes.

There are four starter themes available:

1. **No Code** - For building a theme with the site editor. For theme creators who want to start with an empty theme.

2. **Empty** - This is not a working theme, here you fill in your own empty settings from theme.json. This theme consists of six templates and has no block patterns or styles.

3. **Basic** - Consists of six templates, two template parts and three block patterns and some block styles. Theme.json is partially provided with some global styles.

4. **Advanced** - Consists of seven templates and five template parts. Furthermore, it has seven block patterns and a number of block styles. Theme.json is partially provided with a number of global styles. In addition, the theme is equipped with a number of additional features.

Select a type and use some style options such as colors, initial and width. Then click the **Generate** button.

The *Basic* and *Advanced* themes feature a number of additional files, which allow a theme loads quickly and other protocols function efficiently. You may remove these or leave them in place.

The *No Code* and *Basic* themes are ideal to start with. You may then decide what to add to these.

If you want to add global styles created with Themegen, you can replace the theme.json code.

## Them.es

Go to *https://them.es/starter-fse*.

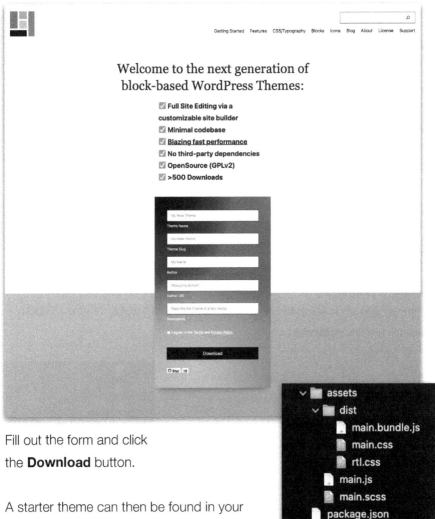

Fill out the form and click
the **Download** button.

A starter theme can then be found in your
download folder. Also included here are some
files that you may leave or delete. The advice
is, if you don't know what it does then it's
better to delete it.

Note! If you delete some files, don't forget to modify the **functions.php** file. Functions containing the name of the deleted file may also be deleted.

See example of a function that may be deleted:

```
18   /**
19    * Add theme support.
20    */
21   function fse_gen_basic_setup() {
22     add_theme_support( 'wp-block-styles' );
23     add_editor_style( './assets/css/style-shared.min.css' );
24
25     /*
26      * Load additional block styles.
27      * See details on how to add more styles in the readme.txt.
28      */
29     $styled_blocks = [ 'button', 'file', 'quote', 'search' ];
30     foreach ( $styled_blocks as $block_name ) {
31       $args = array(
32         'handle' => "fse-gen-basic-$block_name",
33         'src'    => get_theme_file_uri( "assets/css/blocks/$block_name.min.css" ),
34         'path'   => get_theme_file_path( "assets/css/blocks/$block_name.min.css" ),
35       );
36       // Replace the "core" prefix if you are styling blocks from plugins.
37       wp_enqueue_block_style( "core/$block_name", $args );
38     }
39   }
40   add_action( 'after_setup_theme', 'fse_gen_basic_setup' );
41
```

If you want to add global styles created with Themegen, you can replace the theme.json code. Please note, the names of the theme files are obviously not replaced.

# BLOCK THEME PLUGIN

If you have activated a block theme that comes from the WordPress theme library and then changed the **source code**, then after a theme update, all changes are restored. To be clear, these are source code changes, not from the site editor.

To avoid this problem, you can make a theme a Child Theme. In the child theme also called sub theme, you are allowed to completely modify the theme. It inherits all the properties of the main theme. This allows you to change or add features, styles, templates and parts. A theme update does not affect the child theme.

WordPress has now developed a plugin that makes it possible to turn a block theme into a Block Child Theme. The plugin that can be used for this purpose is called **Create Block Theme**. Let's take a look at the different features of this plugin.

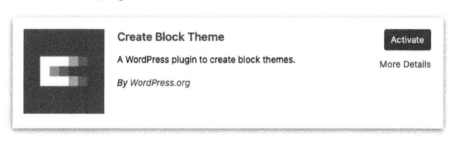

This plugin does more than just create a child theme.
It can also help you further develop your own block theme.
To use the plugin, it is important that you first activate a block theme.

## Install and Activate

Go to **Dashboard > Plugins** and install and activate the **Create Block Theme** plugin.

Then go to **Dashboard > Appearance > Create Block Theme**.

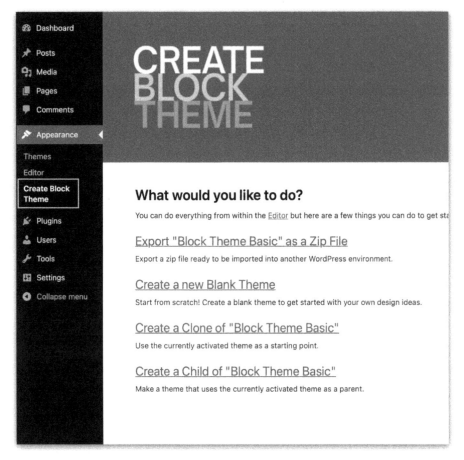

The Dashboard includes **Create Block Theme**. This page will be removed in the next release. You can find these options in the site editor.

Under **Create Block Theme**, you have the following options:

**1. Export ... as a Zip File.**
After adjusting the active theme, you can export it.

**2. Create a new Blank Theme.**
This option creates an blank Starter Theme. This can then be found in the **wp-content > themes** folder of your WordPress installation.
For more info, see chapter *Block Based Starter Theme*.

**3. Create a Clone of ...**
After the theme has been modified, you can use this option to export the theme under a new name. The theme is then no longer dependent on the main theme.

**4. Create a Child of ...**
With this option, you create a Child Theme from the active theme.
Then you can activate and customise the Child Theme. This may also be done under the hood.

## Block theme development

If you have chosen the **Child theme**, **Clone** and **Blank theme** option, a number of fields will appear where you can enter theme information.

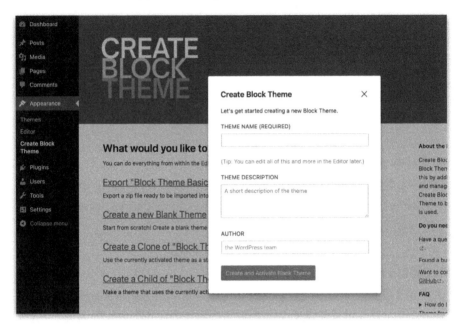

After clicking the **Export ... as a Zip File** button, the theme can be found in the **Downloads** folder. Before developing this further, it must be **installed** and **activated**.

If you have chosen the **Create a new blank theme** option, you can activate it directly from **Dashboard > Appearance > Themes**. The theme folder can be found in the site folder.

On the following pages I'll show you how to apply the plugin.

## Blank theme

1. Make sure a **block theme** is **activated**.
2. Go to **Dashboard > Appearance > Create Block Theme**.
3. Select **Create a new Blank Theme**.
4. Name it **Starter Blank** and fill in the necessary details.
5. Click the **Create and Activate** button.
6. Go to **Dashboard > Appearance > Editor**.
7. Adjust header width. Select **header > Group**, at block options **activate - Inner blocks use content width**. If the Group block does not respond, place the block in an additional Group block.
8. **Footer > paragraph**, align to the left.
9. Then create a navigation menu and click **Save**.

At this stage, it is possible to extend the theme from the Editor, as well as under the hood.

## Theme overwrite

1. Create templates e.g. **single.html** and
   **page.html**. See chapter *Extend block
   theme*. You can **duplicate**, **rename** and
   **modify index.html** for this purpose.
2. Then go to **Dashboard > Editor > Templates**. Open a new page and go to **Create
   Block Theme** (top right) **> Save changes
   to theme > Save Changes**.

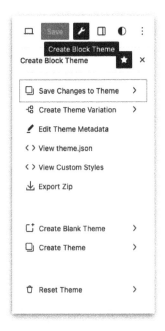

User customizations are deleted with this action.

It is no longer possible to reset theme changes,
see **Editor > Templates > All templates > Actions** (three dots).

From this stage, you can customize and extend the theme with templates
and parts, among other things.

It is also possible to extend the theme under the hood. For example, you
can modify the Toggle Navigation menu, see chapter *Responsive menu*.
When you are ready, use the next option.

## Create style variation

1. Go to **Dashboard > Appearance > Editor > Styles**.
2. At **Styles > Colors** adjust the **background**, **link** and **text color**.

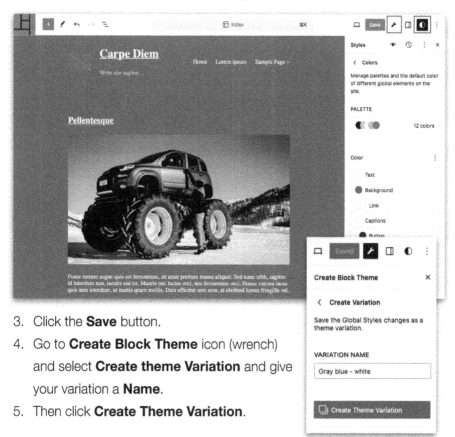

3. Click the **Save** button.
4. Go to **Create Block Theme** icon (wrench) and select **Create theme Variation** and give your variation a **Name**.
5. Then click **Create Theme Variation**.

A confirmation is displayed indicating that a variation has been included in the folder: */Users/name/Local Sites/name_site/app/public/wp-content/themes/blank/styles/gray-blue-white.json*.

Repeat the process to add a new variation.
In this example, the background, link and text color have been adjusted.

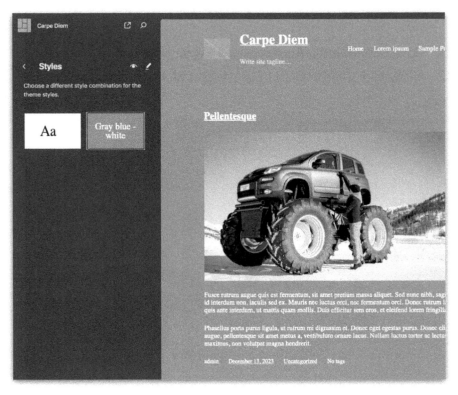

For more variation effect, it is recommended to adjust the typography as well.

When you are done creating variations, it is recommended to **overwrite** the theme again. It is possible that user changes (adjustments from the editor) have been applied in the meantime.

## Export theme

When you are completely done with the theme, you can export it. You can send the final result to the WordPress theme library, for example.

1. From the **site editor**, edit a page and go to **Create Block Theme** (wrench icon).
2. Select the **Export Zip**.
3. The theme can then be found in the **Downloads** folder.

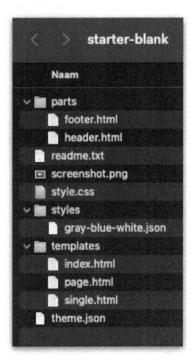

As you have seen, the **Create Block Theme** plugin is a perfect tool to start developing a block theme.

The starter theme contains only the necessary template files. This provides more overview and eliminates the need to figure out the entire structure.

You may also combine it with a theme.json file coming from the block theme generator Themegen.

# SITE EDITOR PLUGINS

The site editor is an integral part of the system. It is user-friendly, generates efficient HTML code and therefore loads quickly in a browser. Meanwhile, there are a number of site editor plugins available that extend the editor with additional blocks and options.

There are also theme builder plugins available, such as Beaver Builder, Bakery or Elementor. Unlike editor plugins, they take the entire site editor after activation. From a proprietary interface, it becomes possible to create a theme. The downside is that they are often not compatible with various WordPress versions, themes and plugins.

A free version is limited and it takes time before you can work with it. A Pro version is expensive, at between $45 and $250 per year. Upon termination of a license, updates are no longer available. In addition, it generates unnecessary HTML code, making the loading time longer than with the standard editor.

The chart below shows the loading speed of WordPress sites created with the Block Editor (Gutenberg) versus various theme builders.

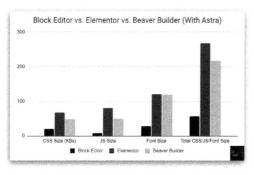

*Speed test 2024, source: onlinemediamasters.com (faster is better).*

As you can see, loading time is faster when a site is created with the default editor. If you miss some options in the editor, you can supplement them with plugins.

These allow you to easily add Google Fonts, a sticky header, animation or other features to a theme. In some cases, you can even turn the visibility of blocks on or off, depending on the screen size. A large number of editor plugins are available for both the site editor and the page editor.

In this chapter, I will show you some plugins that can help you create a block theme:

- Options for Block Themes
- Ghost Kit
- Otter Page Builder
- Twentig
- Editor Beautifier

After a plugin is activated, additional menu items may appear in the dashboard and additional theme blocks and options may be available.

Please note, it is possible that an option may not work with a particular block. In that case, try a different block. Take your time and see what is possible.

## Options for Block Themes

After the plugin is activated, **Theme Options** is included in the dashboard.

**Manage Templates** allows you to manage **templates** and **parts**.
**Theme Options** allows you to **add Google fonts**, activate a **Sticky header** and **Animated Logo**, among others.

After a font is selected, it must still be specified from the site **editor**.
This can be done by adjusting the **Global Style**.

## Ghost Kit

Ghost Kit – Page Builder Blocks & Extensions

Ghost Kit is the powerful page building experience for WordPress.

*By Ghost Kit Team*

Activate

More Details

This is a very versatile plugin. After activation, **Ghostkit** is **included** in the dashboard. In the site editor you will find additional **blocks** such as a **shape divider**, **animation**, **typography** and **options**.

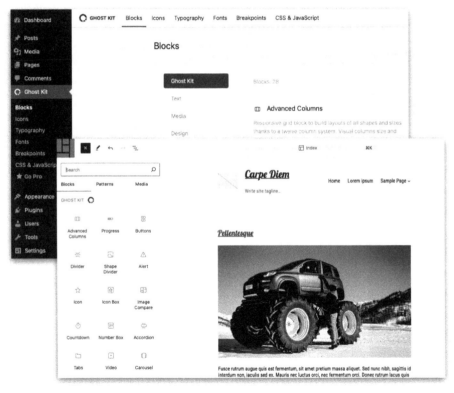

**Ghostkit** is a freemium plugin. A license is required to use all options.

## Otter Page Builder Blocks

After activating the plugin, you will find additional **blocks** such as **Animation**, **Custom CSS** and **options** such as **Visibility Conditions**, among others.

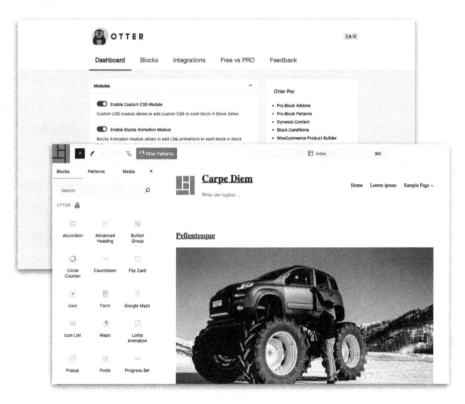

Settings can be found under **Dashboard > Otter Blocks**.

## Twentig

With this plugin you don't get extra blocks, but you do get extra block options. Among other things, it is possible to use **Google fonts**.

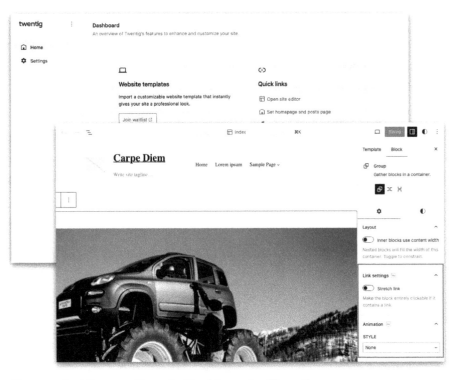

You can find these settings in **Dashboard > Twentig**.

## Editor Beautifier

This plugin displays the structure of a template without using **List View** or **breadcrumbs**.

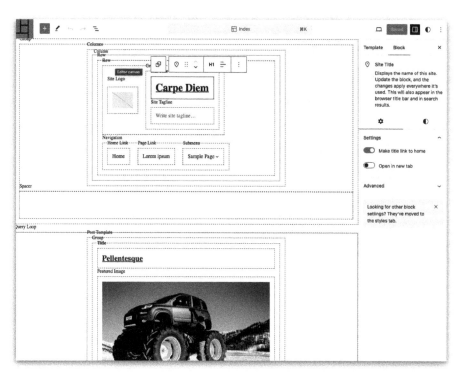

This allows you to select the appropriate block directly from the screen.

# APPLY PLUGINS

Activate the theme **Starter Blank** created using the **Create Block Theme** plugin. See chapter *Block Theme Plugin*. You can also download the theme. After changing the theme, you will **install** and **activate** a plugin.

> **wp-books.com/block-theme**
> **Page 210 - starterblank**

Use plugin: **Ghostkit** for fonts, shape divider and display options.

Tip: Know what you are going to create. To better assess a theme, it is helpful to already include a few pages and posts in a navigation menu. The site features a logo. Pages and posts have a featured image.

## Theme with background image

It is possible to provide a block theme with a background image. For this you can use the **Cover** block. It is even possible to place a complete layout in it.

Go to **Dashboard > Appearance > Editor**.

1. Place a **Cover** block at the top of the template **Index**.
2. **Select** an **image** from the **media library**.
3. From **Toolbar** Cover block - select **Full height**.

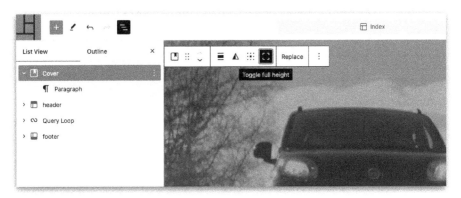

4. Drag **header**, **Query Loop** and **footer** into the **Cover** block.
5. **Remove** the **Paragraph** block from cover block.
6. Replace the **Content** block with the **Excerpt** block.
7. Select **Post template** block. From toolbar select - **Grid view**.
   **Settings > Layout: columns - 3**.

Place the **Query loop** block in a new block **Group**.

Then from **Toolbar** Group - select **Full width**.

Settings **Cover** block- **Styles**:

**Overlay Opacity - 0**.

**Padding** left and right - **0**.

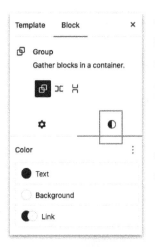

Settings **Group** block -

**Styles**:

**Color: Text** - black.

**Background** - white.

**Header** and **Footer** settings:

**Color Text** - white.

Then go to **Global Styles** (half moon icon) **>
Layout**, and copy the settings.

**Content** 840 px - **Width** 1000 px.

Click **Save** and view the site.

## Ghostkit

After the plugin is installed and activated, additional editor blocks and block options have been added to the system.

Go to the site editor and select the **Header**.
Then go to the block inserter **+** and select the **Shape Divider** block.

After the block is inserted choose the **Style - Tilts** at **block settings**.

**Color** - white.
Go to **Styles > Spacings** (three dots)
**Margin - 0 !**
(Top and Bottom, with exclamation mark **!** ).

Apply the same spacing settings for the
**Group** block.

Repeat the process for an additional shape divider above the **Footer** block.

Click the **Save** button and preview the site.

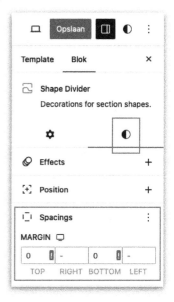

Now to apply a Google font.

Go to **Dashboard > Ghost Kit > Typography**.

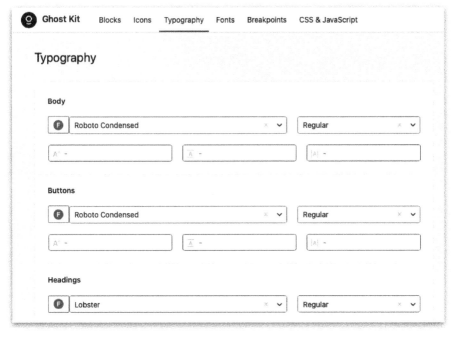

From this screen, select Google fonts for the **Body** (entire site) **Buttons** and **Headings**. The **Show Advanced** button allows you to set the font for each heading. Saving is not necessary.

View the website.

Then a few minor adjustments were made. As you can see, the block **Fill** element as in the header has been removed. The **footer** padding and **Site slogan** margin has been adjusted. The **font size** of the **navigation** menu and header is larger. *Ghostkit* also allows you to use additional block options.

Don't forget to adjust the other templates.

Using the editor and an additional plugin, it is possible to create a theme without technical knowledge. You can also download the theme.

Install the theme from within WordPress. Activate the corresponding plugin. And give the cover image block a background image.

**wp-books.com/block-theme**
**Page 216 - starterblank**

A piece of advice: don't overfill the site editor with plugins. In practice, you only need a small number of additional blocks and options. The range of editor plugins is still limited and these are usually designed for the page editor. After the introduction of the site editor, developers have made some of these features available for Full Site Editing.

To keep up, well-known theme builders nowadays offer editor plugins. These are integrated into the site editor using the Gutenberg user interface. A separate user interface is no longer necessary.

The combination of the site editor and third-party editor blocks creates a consistent interface for creating theme layouts. The best of both worlds.

**Note! If you have finished developing a theme and are going to export it, then the corresponding plugin(s) is part of it.**

In the next chapter, I'll show you how to make this happen.

# THEME WITH PLUGINS

If you want to create a block theme with mandatory and/or recommended plugins, it is useful to make use of a PHP script in your theme.

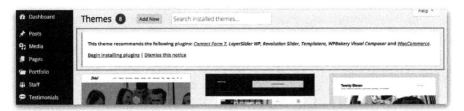

This allows a user, after activating the theme, to quickly and easily install and activate the necessary plugins.

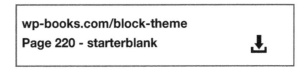

wp-books.com/block-theme
Page 220 - starterblank

A handy method that can help with this is TGM Plugin Activation.

Go to: **tgmpluginactivation.com**. On the next page, you will find instructions on how to add TGM Plugin Activation to the theme.

This program takes care of the installation, updates and activation of one or more mandatory or recommended plugins. It supports embedded plugins as well as plugins from wordpress.org and other providers.

1. Click on menu item **Download**.
2. Enter the theme data. Indicate where you want to apply this code: **Theme**. And how you want to distribute it: **WordPress.org**.

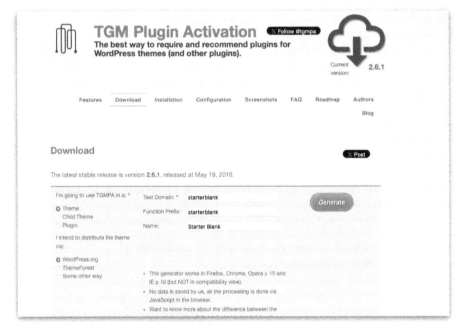

3. Then click the **Generate** button.

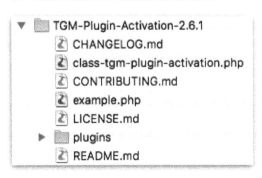

A zip file **tgm-plugin-activa-tion.zip** can be found in the Downloads folder.

4. Unzip the zip file.

Then do the following:

1. Place a copy of the **Starter Blank** theme on your desktop.
2. Place **class-tgm-plugin-activation.php** in the root of the theme.
3. **Open** the file and delete lines 3587 through 3616.

This section is required for a classic theme.

```
3586            */
3587            public function add_strings() {
3588                if ( 'update' === $this->options['install_type'] ) {
3589                    parent::add_strings();
3590                    /* translators: 1: plugin name, 2: action number 3: total number of actions. */
3591                    $this->upgrader->strings['skin_before_update_header'] = __( 'Updating Plugin %1$
3592                } else {
3593                    /* translators: 1: plugin name, 2: error message. */
3594                    $this->upgrader->strings['skin_update_failed_error'] = __( 'An error occurred wh
3595                    /* translators: 1: plugin name. */
3596                    $this->upgrader->strings['skin_update_failed'] = __( 'The installation of %1$s f

3598                    if ( $this->tgmpa->is_automatic ) {
3599                        // Automatic activation strings.
3600                        $this->upgrader->strings['skin_upgrade_start'] = __( 'The installation and act
     •                      patient.', 'tgmpa' );
3601                        /* translators: 1: plugin name. */
3602                        $this->upgrader->strings['skin_update_successful'] = __( '%1$s installed and a
     •                      onclick="%2$s"><span>' . esc_html__( 'Show Details', 'tgmpa' ) . '</span><span
3603                        $this->upgrader->strings['skin_upgrade_end']          = __( 'All installations an
3604                        /* translators: 1: plugin name, 2: action number 3: total number of actions. *
3605                        $this->upgrader->strings['skin_before_update_header'] = __( 'Installing and Ac
3606                    } else {
3607                        // Default installation strings.
3608                        $this->upgrader->strings['skin_upgrade_start'] = __( 'The installation process
     •                      );
3609                        /* translators: 1: plugin name. */
3610                        $this->upgrader->strings['skin_update_successful'] = esc_html__( '%1$s install
     •                      . esc_html__( 'Show Details', 'tgmpa' ) . '</span><span class="hidden">' . esc
3611                        $this->upgrader->strings['skin_upgrade_end']          = __( 'All installations ha
3612                        /* translators: 1: plugin name, 2: action number 3: total number of actions. *
3613                        $this->upgrader->strings['skin_before_update_header'] = __( 'Installing Plugin
3614                    }
3615                }
3616            }
3617
```

4. Place **example.php** in the root of the theme and change the name to **starterblank_plugins.php**.
5. **Open** the file and modify the path, line 34 :

```
 * Plugin:
 * require_once dirname( __FILE__ ) . '/path/to/class-tgm-plugin-activation.php';
 */
require_once get_template_directory() . '/class-tgm-plugin-activation.php';
```

## 6. Then delete lines 62 to 91.

```
61
62    // This is an example of how to include a plugin bundled with a theme.
63    array(
64       'name'             => 'TGM Example Plugin', // The plugin name.
65       'slug'             => 'tgm-example-plugin', // The plugin slug (typically the folder name).
66       'source'           => get_template_directory() . '/lib/plugins/tgm-example-plugin.zip', // The plugin source
67       'required'         => true, // If false, the plugin is only 'recommended' instead of required.
68       'version'          => '', // E.g. 1.0.0. If set, the active plugin must be this version or higher. If the pl
  .   will be notified to update the plugin.
69       'force_activation'   => false, // If true, plugin is activated upon theme activation and cannot be deactivate
70       'force_deactivation' => false, // If true, plugin is deactivated upon theme switch, useful for theme-specific
71       'external_url'     => '', // If set, overrides default API URL and points to an external URL.
72       'is_callable'      => '', // If set, this callable will be be checked for availability to determine if a plu
73    ),
74
75    // This is an example of how to include a plugin from an arbitrary external source in your theme.
76    array(
77       'name'         => 'TGM New Media Plugin', // The plugin name.
78       'slug'         => 'tgm-new-media-plugin', // The plugin slug (typically the folder name).
79       'source'       => 'https://s3.amazonaws.com/tgm/tgm-new-media-plugin.zip', // The plugin source.
80       'required'     => true, // If false, the plugin is only 'recommended' instead of required.
81       'external_url' => 'https://github.com/thomasgriffin/New-Media-Image-Uploader', // If set, overrides default AP
82    ),
83
84    // This is an example of how to include a plugin from a GitHub repository in your theme.
85    // This presumes that the plugin code is based in the root of the GitHub repository
86    // and not in a subdirectory ('/src') of the repository.
87    array(
88       'name'     => 'Adminbar Link Comments to Pending',
89       'slug'     => 'adminbar-link-comments-to-pending',
90       'source'   => 'https://github.com/jrfnl/WP-adminbar-comments-to-pending/archive/master.zip',
91    ),
92
```

## 7. Below that you will find comments: `// This is … Plugin Repository.` Here you can specify which plugins are used.

```
// This is an example of how to include a plugin from the WordPress Plugin Re
array(
   'name'       => 'BuddyPress',
   'slug'       => 'buddypress',
   'required'   => false,
),

// This is an example of the use of 'is_callable' functionality. A user could
// have WPSEO installed *or* WPSEO Premium. The slug would in that last case
// 'wordpress-seo-premium'.
// By setting 'is_callable' to either a function from that plugin or a class
// `array( 'class', 'method' )` similar to how you hook in to actions and fil
// recognize the plugin as being installed.
array(
   'name'         => 'WordPress SEO by Yoast',
   'slug'         => 'wordpress-seo',
   'is_callable'  => 'wpseo_init',
),
```

The file uses two plugins, BuddyPress and SEO Yoast. These are included in the WordPress.org library.

8. Replace these for **Hello Dolly** and **Ghostkit**, see image.

```
// This is an example of how to include a plugin from the WordPress Plugin Reposito
array(
    'name'      => 'Hello Dolly',
    'slug'      => 'hello-dolly',
    'required'  => true,
),
// This is an example of how to include a plugin from the WordPress Plugin Reposito
array(
    'name'      => 'Ghostkit',
    'slug'      => 'ghostkit',
    'required'  => true,
),
```

`'required => true'` - plugin is required.

`'required => false'` - plugin is recommended.

9. At `* Array of configuration settings…` you will find a number of settings. Copy the settings below.

```
/*
 * Array of configuration settings. Amend each line as needed.
 *
 * TGMPA will start providing localized text strings soon. If you already have translations of our standard
 * strings available, please help us make TGMPA even better by giving us access to these translations or by
 * sending in a pull-request with .po file(s) with the translations.
 *
 * Only uncomment the strings in the config array if you want to customize the strings.
 */
$config = array(
    'id'            => 'starterblank',          // Unique ID for hashing notices for multiple instances of TGMPA.
    'default_path'  => '',                      // Default absolute path to bundled plugins.
    'menu'          => 'tgmpa-install-plugins', // Menu slug.
    'parent_slug'   => 'themes.php',            // Parent menu slug.
    'capability'    => 'edit_theme_options',    // Capability needed to view plugin install page, should be a capability a
    'has_notices'   => true,                    // Show admin notices or not.
    'dismissable'   => false,                   // If false, a user cannot dismiss the nag message.
    'dismiss_msg'   => 'Om het theme te gebruiken zijn de onderstaande plugins verplicht.',    // If 'dismissable' is fal
    'is_automatic'  => true,                    // Automatically activate plugins after installation or not.
    'message'       => 'Selecteer alle plugins. Kies voor Bulkacties > Install, klik daarna op de knop toepassen<br /> ',
```

10. Then **save** the file.

11. Open **functions.php** and insert the code below:

```
/**
 * tgm-plugin-activation
 */
require get_template_directory() . '/starterblank_plugins.php';
```

12. **Save** file.

To see if it works, go install the theme in a new WordPress installation.

After the theme is installed go to **Dashboard > Appearance > Themes** and **activate** the theme, **Starter Blank**.

As is indicated, the theme requires two plugins.

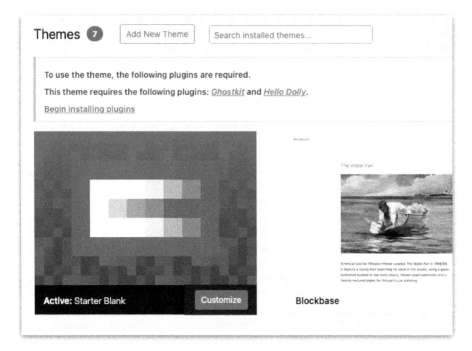

Click **Begin installing plugin**. **Select** all plugins.

Select the **Install** option. Then click the **Apply** button.

The plugins are installed and updated, then a confirmation is displayed.

View site.

# FUTURE OF BLOCK THEMES

With the Gutenberg **page editor**, it became possible to easily add layout to pages and posts.

With the advent of the **site editor**, it is possible to customize a theme in the same way. At least, that was the intention.... Meanwhile, the site editor has evolved into a **site builder**.

Creating a WordPress block theme does not require any programming knowledge. Default features are included, such as a responsive menu and layout blocks. Editor plugins allow you to add additional functionality to a theme.

Creating a classic theme is not easy. It requires a lot of programming know-ledge. All functionality is included in a theme, which results in a large number of files and a higher chance of errors.

Thanks to the new block method, this process is faster. The focus is more on the visual aspect and usability of a theme. A perfect tool for web designers, making them less dependent on web developers.

**The arrival of the site editor is a Game Changer.**

If you have no programming knowledge, delve into markup languages such as HTML and CSS. Use editor plugins only when you really need them.

Look at other block themes, too. This will increase your knowledge and understanding.

With additional programming knowledge, you are not dependent on the site editor and plugins. Under the hood, you can make quick adjustments and additions. These types of themes are generally secure, efficient, lightweight and fast.

As you've seen, the site editor is a big step forward.
It gives a different perspective on creating WordPress websites.

The advice I can give you is: know what you are going to create, sketch the layout first and decide what features you want to apply. Use the list view and breadcrumbs to select the right blocks. There are plenty of options to style all the blocks.

What else can we expect? Improvement and expansion of the editor, more patterns, blocks, options, plugins and **more block themes**.

The future looks bright.
I hope you have fun creating WordPress block themes !

# INFORMATION

If you want to know more about the development of block themes, there are a number of websites and blogs you can keep an eye on.

## WordPress
*wordpress.org/news*
*developer.wordpress.org/themes*

## Gutenberg block, plugins and themes reference
*wp-a2z.org*
*github.com/WordPress*

## Template builder
*gutenberghub.com/introducing-gutenberg-template-builder*
*themegen.app*
*them.es/starter-fse*

## Blog Full Site Editing
*fullsiteediting.com*
*themeshaper.com*
*gutenberghub.com*
*gutenbergtimes.com*

# ABOUT THE WRITER

### Roy Sahupala, multimedia-specialist

*"Multimedia specialist is just a title. In addition to creating multimedia products, I have been giving web design training for more than 26 years and continue to love it when people get excited by being able to do much more in a short time than they thought possible beforehand."*

After studying industrial design, Roy trained as a multimedia specialist. He then gained experience at several multimedia agencies. In 2000, he founded his own company, WJAC (With Jazz and Conversations), which specializes in creating multimedia products for various clients and advertising agencies.

Since 2001, in addition to his work, Roy has also been active as a instructor and has set up various web design training courses in cooperation with educational institutions.

WordPress books written by Roy Sahupala:

Explore WordPress books at *wp-books.com*.